Mukundh Bhushan

BLUEROSE PUBLISHERS
India | U.K.

Copyright © Mukundh Bhushan 2024

All rights reserved by author. No part of this publication may be reproduced, stored in a retrieval system or transmitted in any form or by any means, electronic, mechanical, photocopying, recording or otherwise, without the prior permission of the author. Although every precaution has been taken to verify the accuracy of the information contained herein, the publisher assumes no responsibility for any errors or omissions. No liability is assumed for damages that may result from the use of information contained within.

BlueRose Publishers takes no responsibility for any damages, losses, or liabilities that may arise from the use or misuse of the information, products, or services provided in this publication.

For permissions requests or inquiries regarding this publication, please contact:

BLUEROSE PUBLISHERS
www.BlueRoseONE.com
info@bluerosepublishers.com
+91 8882 898 898
+4407342408967

ISBN: 978-93-5989-006-7

Cover Design: Mukundh Bhushan
Typesetting: Mukundh Bhushan

First Edition: June 2024

~~Forward~~

Foreword

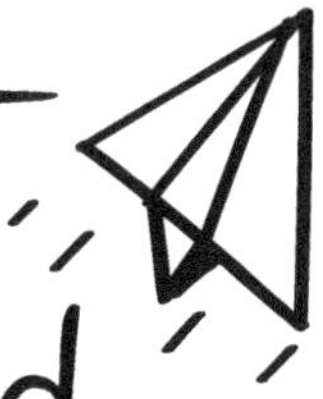

—·—·—·—·—·—·—·—·—·—·—·—·—·—·

The author of this book Think the Luna Way has given a modest representation how startups begin their journey from idea generation giving a vision to how certainties and uncertainties can drive the overall journey with the question HOW? The word HOW has been applied practically.

As the journey sinks in the Chapter 2, give about WHAT and WHY further giving a path to understand the four phases of Design – Incept, Devise, Encompass, and Architect. This opens up into Amazing IDEA as a reference point.

Chapter 3, describes the six design phases which begins with a brainstorming session consisting of different sub phases. Overall, this chapter will give you a holistic view of the real time processes. This begins with a Alone Time.

Chapter 3a and 3b, the different stages of Design LUNA and Feed the FORM are discussed giving the book more strength to solve every facet of the stages a STARTUP goes through. Overall, these Chapters give you the ingredients to develop a STARTUP and progress toward being a VISIONARY which is one of the corporate requirements and how quickly these ideas are transformed into product or service to stay in the market.

— Dr. Chakrapani Gopal

—·—·—·—·—·—·—·—·—·—·—·—·—·—·

Hi Dr. Chakrapani Gopal! Could I know more about you?

Sure! here goes...

I have a total dual experience of 25 years. I served in many industry verticals maximum time with most of my hours in the IT industry. I worked in academia for around 7 years as Researcher, Head Academics and as a Coordinator for MBA Programs at various business schools.

What are you upto these days?

In the year 2022 I returned back to the the corporate world! I currently work with an IT software services and consulting organization.

Tell me something interesting about you?

I have co authored 2 books "Supply Chain Management" and "Microenterprises and Business Communication Handbook for Microentrepreneurs"

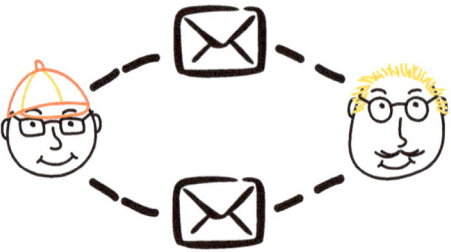

Table of Contents

Chapter 1: Introduction 1

Chapter 2: Design LUNA 15

Chapter 3: Stages of Design LUNA 27

    Chapter 3[a]: Stages of Design LUNA/ Gear up! 31

    Chapter 3[b]: Stages of Design LUNA/ Feed the Storm 47

    Chapter 3[c]: Stages of Design LUNA/ Get...Set...Go! 73

Chapter 4: Cool as ICE 119

From LOST to Design LUNA 139

Destiny: Design LUNA 219

About the Author 287

Chapter 1
Introduction

Ring *Ring*
Hey there!

Are you filled with so many ideas and way too overwhelmed to figure out how to start?

~~or~~

Are you a master of your mind and sharpening your creative and thinking abilities...

Then you are in for a treat...

💡 Did you know?

We get over 185,000 thoughts per month, and one of these thoughts is the NEXT BIG THING!

Each of them an unique idea

And distinct paths to implement

And plenty of destinations to reach

Each, an *exciting* journey and story in their own right...

How will that one special idea become the ONE!

How... How... How... Let's figure out "HOW"?

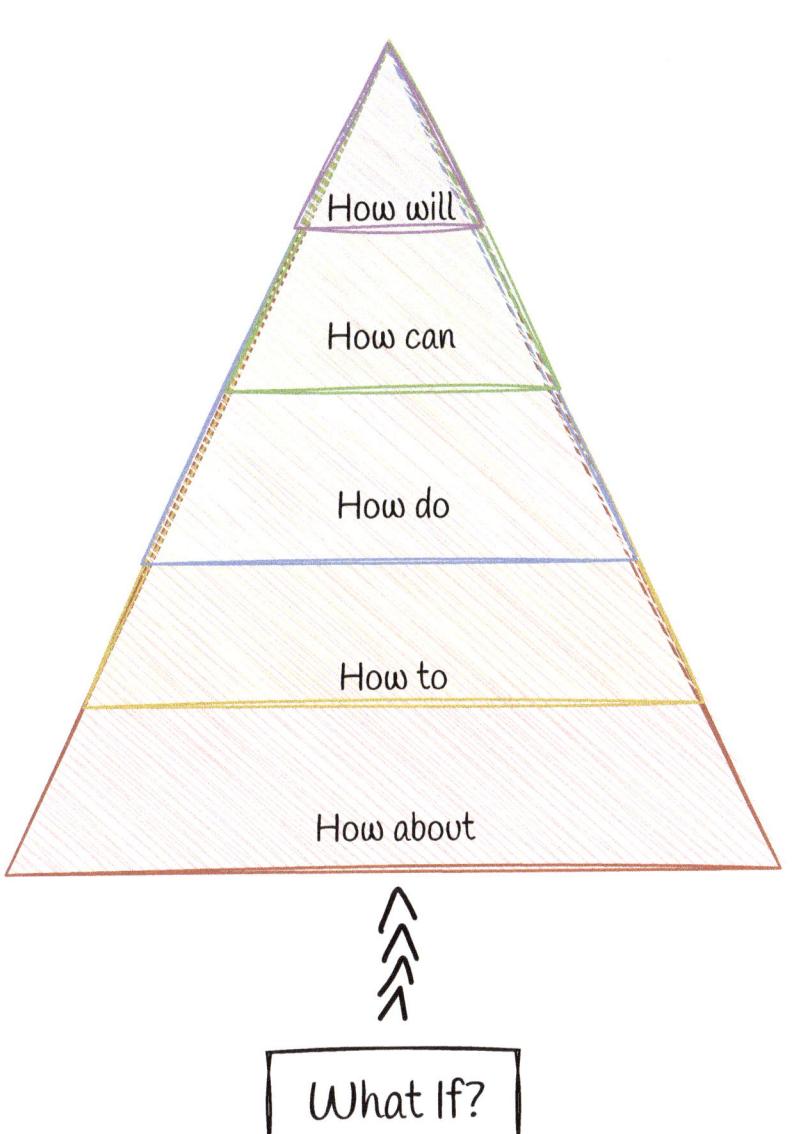

What are all these "how"s?

Recognize Opportunity

This step is where you recognize a potential opportunity as your idea...

"What if" there is an easier way to process my payments

"What if" there is some way to collaborate with all of my employees

"What if" there is a channel to learn specific skills

Problem know how

Here you identify potential avenues in the space around your idea...

"How about" connecting my card to my mobile?

"How about" a payment gateway to process my transactions?

"How about" a SMS to complete payment in rural areas?

Starting trouble

Here you figure out ways to get the ball rolling for the Idea...

"How to" gather intel for this idea?

"How to" get people interested for this idea?

"How to" protect my idea?

Operation problem

Here you are thinking of ways to kick start the work/ operations...

"How do" I get started?

"How do" I run my business?

"How do" I find the right investors?

Improve core idea

Here you build on your core USP to keep up with the competition...

Unique Selling Point

"How can" I keep my customers glued with my Idea?

"How can" my business scale faster?

"How can" I keep up with the latest trends?

Expand idea

Your idea has now seen the light of day and is doing great! How will you expand your Idea?

"How will" I go global?

"How will" I improve customer interactions?

"How will" I integrate with other products ?

Too many twists and turns like a maze... isn't it?

Bring your idea to light....

IDEA

Now, it's time to meet someone special...

Notes:

Notes:

Notes:

Chapter 2

Design LUNA

Design LUNA
~~Revise~~ Improvise...

What is Design LUNA?

Design LUNA is a generalized thinking process that not only focuses on the solution part but also the problem at hand, and the new ones that pop-up along the way. It can be used from a wide variety of tasks, from something as simple as trying out your own masterchef recipe to your billion dollar startup idea that could change the world.

Why we Designed LUNA?

We, at Threadality technologies, love finding solutions to problems and building new stuff.

In this pursuit, we like pushing ourselves to travel in paths lesser known.

It was through analyzing these experiences, thought process and our approach, we were able to identify patterns. This in turn led us to formulate "Design LUNA".

Before bringing this book to you... we tested it on different verticals and fine-tuned this process!

Why LUNA?

"Luna" is considered as one of the most beautiful moths in nature...

Why moth? aren't butterflies the way to go?

Processes are something which typically need to be adhered to... so... not so fancy as a butterfly... right...

But our Luna finds the perfect balance between you being creative and you thinking analytically!

4 Phases of Design LUNA

These form the backbone for your amazing IDEA...

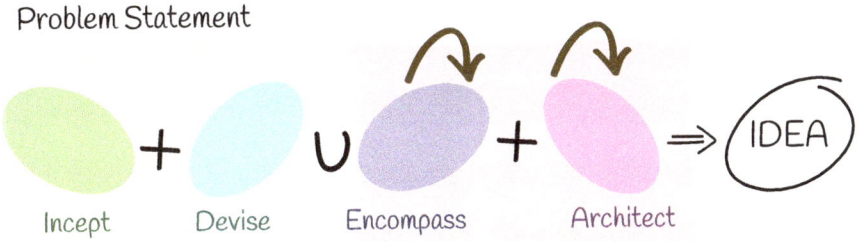

The most important step...often overlooked :(

Let's map our wings with the "Pyramid of How"

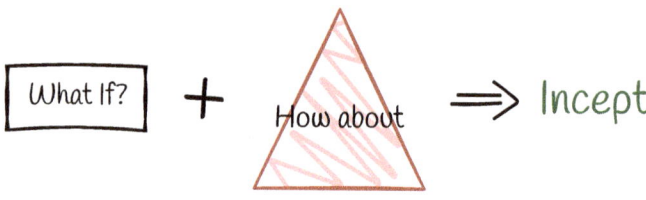

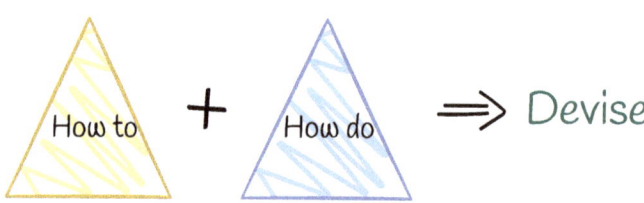

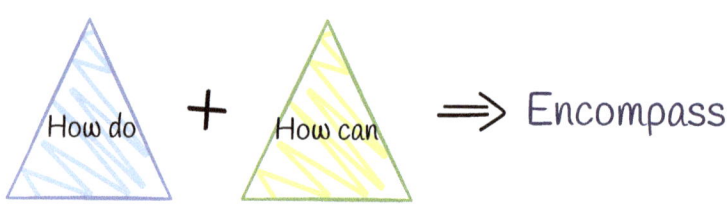

Wait! briefing first!

Sketch out your month with LUNA like this...

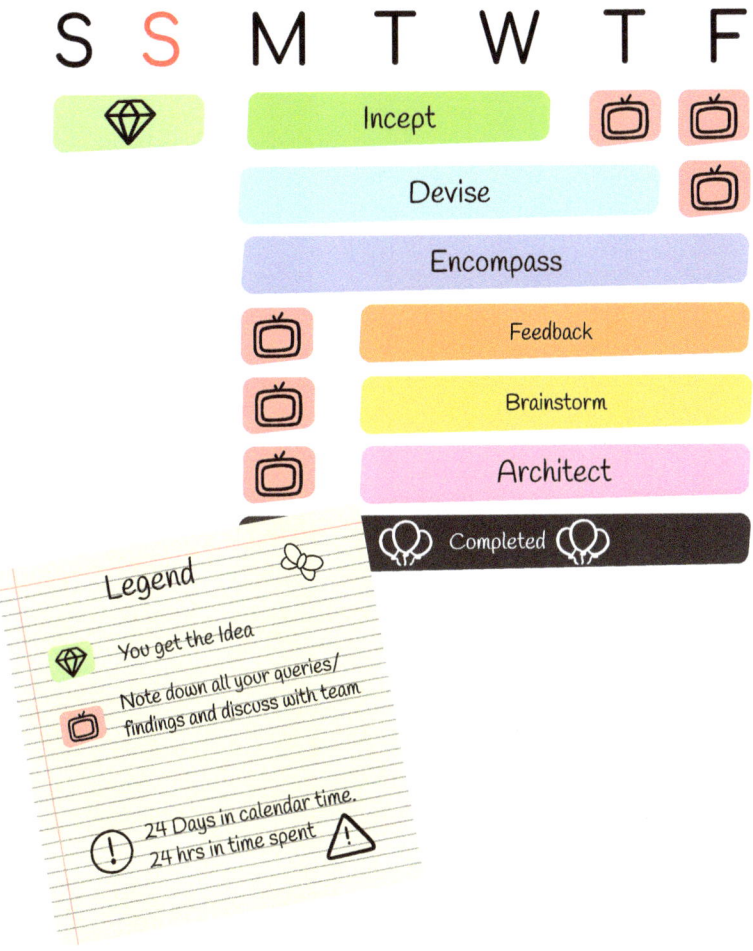

During each of the 4 phases of Design LUNA, you will be performing these activities:

Think → Assemble → Communicate → Develop

Keep the *dialogue* flowing and make it as interactive as possible!

Now let's set the "Stage"...

Notes:

Notes:

Notes:

Notes:

Chapter 3

Stages of Design LUNA

Stage Layout in LUNA

Each wing of the moth luna represents a phase which acts as a milestone...

Now... Under each phase there is a "Stage" followed by an intermediary stage called "Bridge", which helps you to advance to the next "Stage".

Better explained in the illustration below

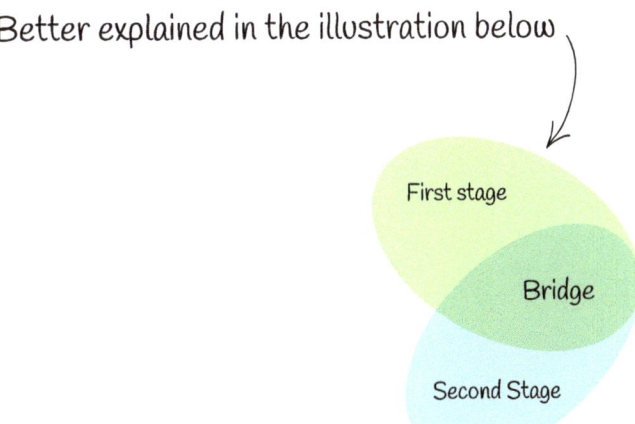

Just like your favourite movie, novel or maybe a play...

Each "Stage" helps you to build your idea like how a character is built!

Successfully completing a stage adds to your progress and a chance to pat your back!

Stages of Design LUNA

Behold the 6 stages!

Starting with 'Alone time' where you think...

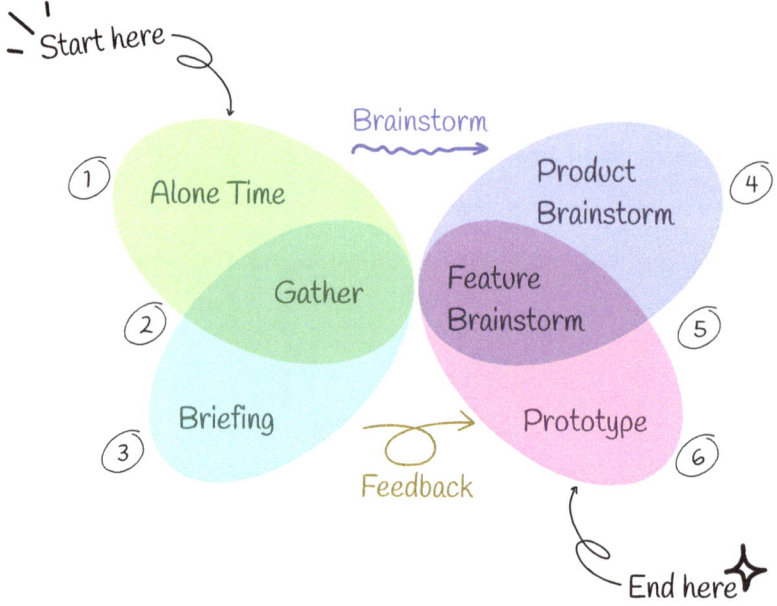

...End with 'Prototype' NOT pilot where you structure your solution

Now Off to the first Stage

Chapter 3ª

Stages of Design LUNA/
Gear up!

Problem Statement

① Alone Time

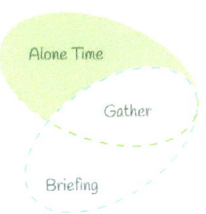

The First stage of many to come. If it is your idea, this step is for you.

Understand the problem you are trying to solve... better!

Get wild with your idea and possible solutions which come up in your head.

Try to be as free-minded as possible, do not restrict yourself.

Tip from Luna #1
Create an inspiring environment for yourself. Nature is the best way to go. Maybe go for a walk, so many things you could notice and incorporate to your idea!

Describe your problem statement as detailed as possible, with no direct references to the solutions.

Write down the problem statement in 1-2 lines, this way you understand the important pain points.

Note down all the different types of stakeholders who are part of your idea.

In this step you are trying to cover all the possible avenues and discover new ones.

Tip from Luna #2
Play scenarios of each of the stakeholder and how each of them interact with your idea. Create a tabulation of all the pitfalls and benefits you identified in this process.

This is your time no good or bad ideas just (ideas!!)

② Gather

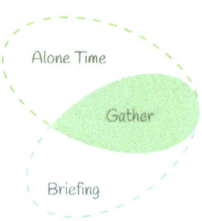

Although this process can be done alone... LUNA works best with a group of people as diverse as possible to get inputs from different backgrounds and cultures.

The People Pool

Upto 10 members would work just fine. Start by making a list of 3 people you think need to be a part and then they suggest 2 people each.

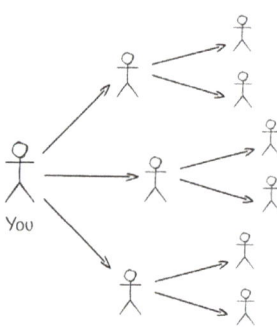

Tip from Luna #3

Make sure each of the suggested people are from different divisions or backgrounds

 Give each of the participants as little information as possible about the idea!

 Now, channel the inner event manager in you!

Decide on the following:

>>>> Meeting place

>>>> Time

>>>> Agenda

Tip from Luna #4

Make sure the meeting place is somewhere which inspires the members

LUNA think kit:

Before the meeting starts you need to "Gather" the following:

One of this
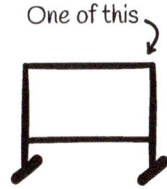

Board:
This could be a white board or a projection which all the participants get to see at all times.

One of this

Stop watch:
To time each participant's turn.

Each bring their own

Noting device:
A notebook, iPad or a similar device to note down points being discussed.

One of this

A talking Stick:
An object which needs to be passed around and the one who posses it would talk, the others listen.

Oh no!

Where is your cap?

How are you going to think?

No problem! let's just make one!

Follow these simple steps.

All you need is a sheet of paper

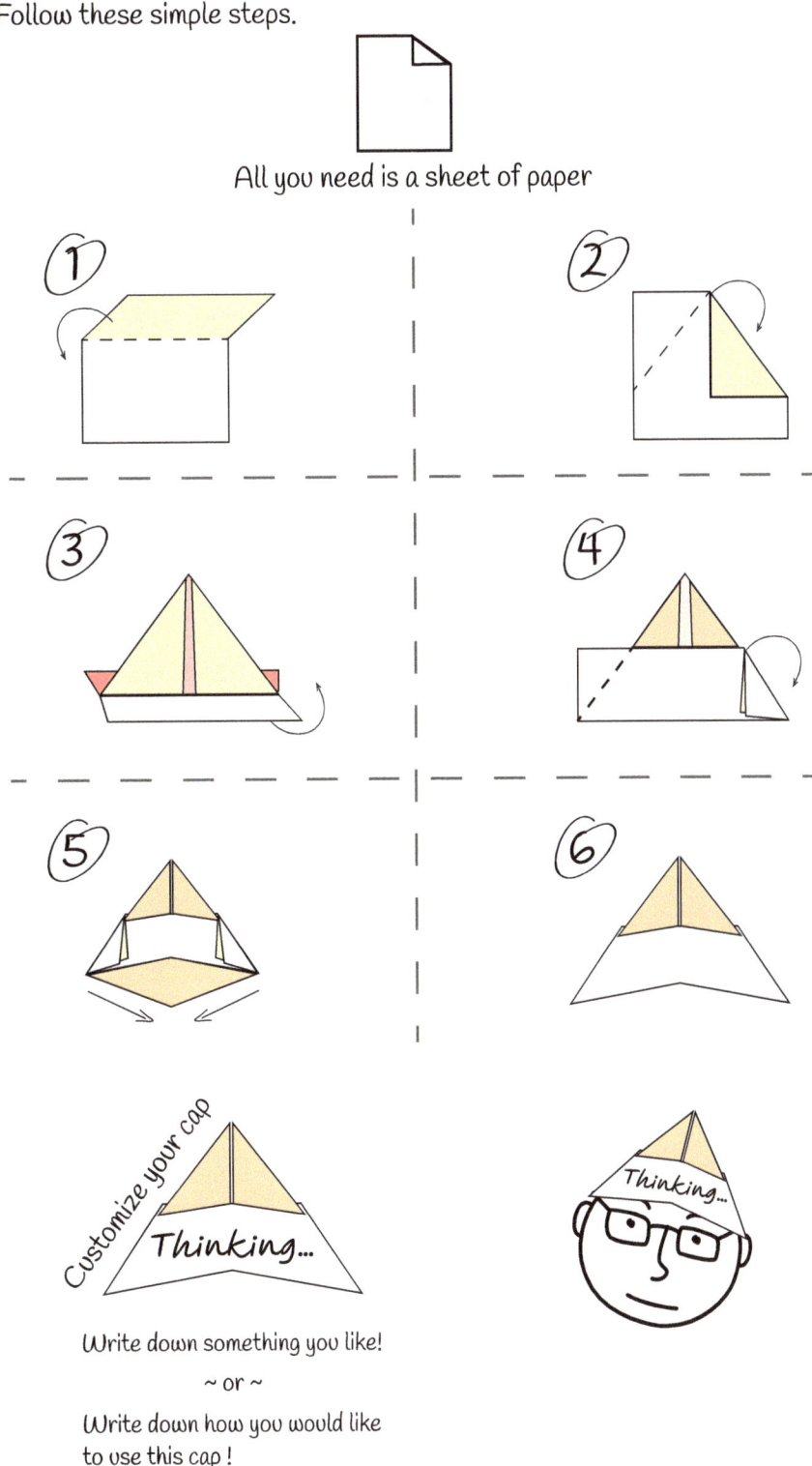

① ② ③ ④ ⑤ ⑥

Customize your cap

Thinking...

Write down something you like!

~ or ~

Write down how you would like to use this cap!

Why not
Make a talking stick as well!

You will be needing only one of this by the way!

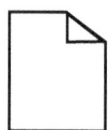

All you need is a sheet of paper

Follow these simple steps.

①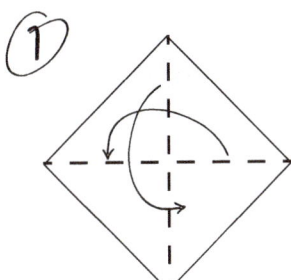

Make a crease by folding and unfold again

②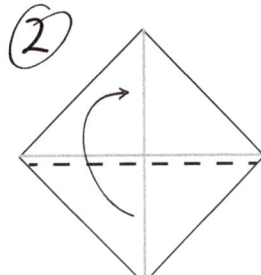

Fold along the new dotted line

③

Your paper must look something like this.
Now turn the paper around

④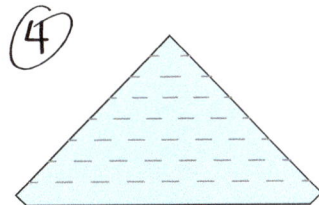

Roll the paper up

⑤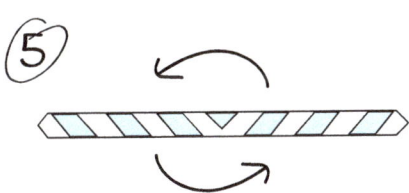

Your paper must look something like this.
Now turn the paper around again

⑥

Fold the paper along the dotted lines

⑦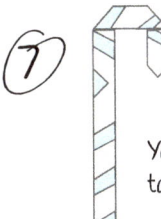

Yay! You have a cool candy talking stick!

Stages of Design LUNA

③ Briefing

Write your problem statement and "Idea" on the white board

Problem statement
Write down the 1 line description about the problem statement.

The Idea
A one line description of the idea you (as creator) have come up with.

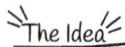

Participants get 5 mins to read and analyze both lines

Story Time

This is a good time to tell your thought behind the idea.

A story will always make people more attached and understand the problem better.

Tip from Luna #5
DO NOT prepare your story before hand or during 'Alone time'. Spontaneity brings true emotion and pain points than a scripted one!

The screenplay

Wrap-up your story in 5 mins max!
Your story must contain the following acts:

Tip from Luna #6
After your story, on the board, note down all key points and give them their act name.

This will help you and the participants to better break down the idea.

 1) What were you trying to do
 2) What you required
 3) The action you took
 4) Problem you faced during execution
 5) Outcome of the action you took
 6) Consequence
 7) Proposed solution
 8) Why it might be useful
 9) Compare

Stages of Design LUNA

A very heart touching story

My mother and I were trying to bake a cake for my father's birthday before he came back from work. ←

We searched for a bit and found the recipe for the cake he loves the most. We made a list of the ingredients required. ←

After we double-checked, we were off to the store. ←

We could only find few of the ingredients not all of them. We jumped from store to store until we found all the ingredients. ←

We were very exhausted and almost had no time to complete the cake before he came home. ←

We hurried and made the cake but we were not totally satisfied by it. ←

Then it occurred to me to create an app where you could look up all of your groceries, order them through it, and have them delivered right to your door. ←

This would have saved a lot of time as we could have pre heated the oven or decorated the house in the mean time. ←

Before me and my mother had to run around to find all the ingredients we need, with this app all you need to do is search and then the groceries are at your door step. ←

 Curtain closes

 A quick 2 mins Q & A, if required

No detailed Questions... just generic ones.

 You are not brain storming yet!

Notes:

Notes:

Notes:

Notes:

Chapter 3ᵇ

Stages of Design LUNA/
Feed the Storm

A Bridge for a Bridge?

Oh wait! 2 bridges?

Before we move to the next stages of LUNA we need to go over 2 very important things:

Feedback

Brainstorming

Very important steps which from now on you and your team will be utilizing lot more!

We suggest conducting a round of  feedback the LUNA way after every stage from now on.

Especially after product brainstorm and feature brainstorm stages.

Let's first start off with

Feedback

 # Feedback the LUNA way!

One of the most important step in your product design and development stages

In design LUNA we split the crowd who provide feedback into 2 segments:

Biased crowd   Unbiased crowd.

Its important to obtain feedback from both these crowds to get a broader understanding!

Biased crowd

Biased crowd in our case is the crowd which was part of the LUNA session in one or the other.

This team worked on the product, so will have a different outlook and understating compared to others.

==Utilize this crowd to understand how an user who has been using the product for a long time would think and navigate==

Unbiased crowd

People who are not part of the LUNA session in any way possible.

This crowd has no clue about what you and your idea are upto. This crowd would help you better understand the pain points, pit falls in design or maybe even a pitch, if you would like to pitch it to an investor later on.

==This crowd will help you better understand easy of use and depth of initial understanding==

We now know the crowds... Now let's figure out how to utilize them! through Personas...

Personas

 Time to put on your feedCap!/acting cap!

The person collecting the feedback must play different roles to better understand and analyze the feedback received...

The Journalist

The Negotiator

The Closer

1) The Journalist

Your job here is to ask questions and note down the points raised by first "the biased" and then "the unbiased" crowd... that's it!

 You are not challenging any view points yet!

Collect all the information you can and discuss with your team.

Repeat this process until you think you and your team have collected enough information.

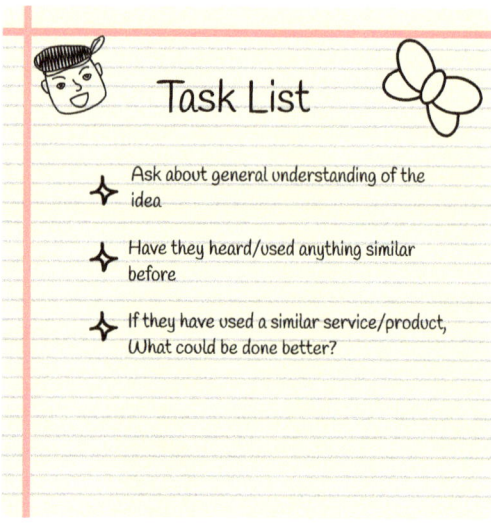

Task List

- Ask about general understanding of the idea
- Have they heard/used anything similar before
- If they have used a similar service/product, What could be done better?

② The Negotiator

At this point you must have filtered all the data collected from the previous role.

Better questioning

You need to frame your questions with:

"Why not" — "What If"

for Biased crowd — for unbiased crowd

>>>> This activity is to be done within your team <<<<

The 'why not' questions must be framed with the points gathered from the previous step.

Here, you get to strike a conversation with the biased crowd.

Frame your 'why not' questions using the points or confusions the unbiased crowd had during the previous step!

Why not? <unbiased crowd point>

For instance "why not sell it online?"

~~OR~~

Why not? <unbiased crowd confusion>

For instance "why not just call the store?"

*Referring to the grocery application

 What if? ⟹ Un-Biased crowd

>>>> This activity can be done within your team but we suggest to speak with a set of unbiased crowd <<<<

Similar to the "why not" questions, the "what if" questions must be framed with the points gathered from "The journalist" step.

 You are going to do the opposite

Here you get to strike a conversation with the unbiased crowd.

Frame your why not question using the points or clarifications the biased crowd came up with during the previous step!

Why not? \<Biased crowd point\>

For instance "What if we showcase it in an exhibition"

Why not? \<Biased crowd clarification\>

For instance "What if you don't have the store's number?

By the end of this activity you should be able to:

Understand the pitfalls. Use this opportunity to figure out ways to address these pitfalls and maybe even tweak your ideas a bit, if required!

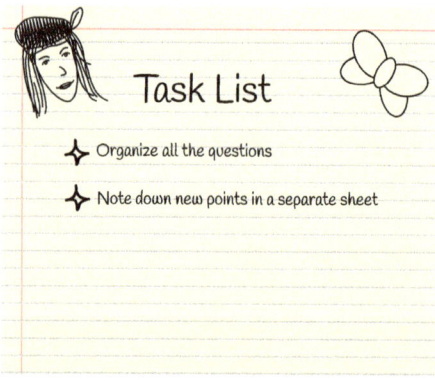

Task List
- Organize all the questions
- Note down new points in a separate sheet

③ The Closer

 Time to feel all suited up like Harvey Spector.

This activity is mostly done with in your team.

Now with all the information collected, pit falls raised and confusions which arised from the biased and unbiased group; you and your team sort out:

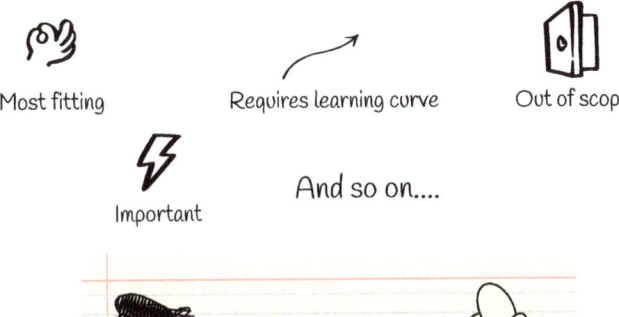

- Most fitting
- Requires learning curve
- Out of scope
- Important
- And so on....

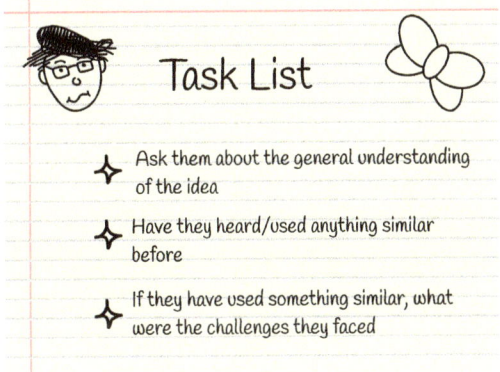

Task List
- Ask them about the general understanding of the idea
- Have they heard/used anything similar before
- If they have used something similar, what were the challenges they faced

 Collecting feedback is not a one step process, you might have to revisit the design phase or the architect phase a number of times before your idea is ready to be implemented.

Ufff! that was a lot of work!
Now the fun part!
Let's first start off with

Brainstorming

Notes:

Notes:

Notes:

Brainstorm the LUNA way

 Before we jump right into Brainstorming
Here are the How's & and the What's we need to address

Brainstorming in LUNA is split into 2 states

The Excited Kid state

In this state you are an unstoppable force. Every idea is great and worth looking into.

The Grumpy Uncle state

All good things come to an end and you need to get back to reality. In this state, you will filter the great ideas from the good and the ones which did not make the cut.

Let's get the setup out of the way first

First off... you will be needing:

1 Facilitator:

(Preferably the person who came up with "the Idea".)
Facilitator will note down all the Ideas being thrown around. Makes sure each participant gets a chance and the determined time is followed for each of the participants. The facilitator can participate in the Brainstorming session as well!

2 Participants:

Everyone who were chosen during the "Gather" phase.

Participants well... need to participate. Put on your thinking caps, Throw ideas around, make the session as fruitful as possible.

 Flashback to the "Gather" Phase

Uses this — One of this
Board

Uses this — One of this
Stop watch

Each bring their own
Common for all

One of this
Common for all

Setting rules for your Brainstorming session

Time for each participant • How long would each session be • To each their own
Prevent grouping within the group.

Sessions during your Bainstroming

① Air — ② Water — ③ Rock

Here you encapsulate all the ideas and come up with a solid final product which you will be using for rest of the steps and development as well!

The core brainstorming session.

Bring lot more structure to the ideas. Be flexible with time!

Here all the participants have a fresh mind and have no influence because of others ideas. Let this session have lesser time allocated.

→ Go this way!

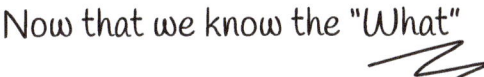

Now that we know the "What"

Let's device a plan to make the brainstorming session more effective.

First off

Every participant gets their own alone time for around 5 mins (or choose how ever long you want it to be 10 mins max)

Let each of the participant understand how they would look at the problem and device solutions accordingly.

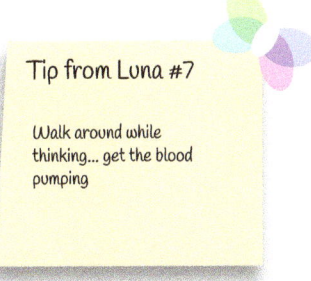

Tip from Luna #7

Walk around while thinking... get the blood pumping

Note down all your solutions, maybe you think an app will do the trick, or maybe you thought of a feature which could be added, or you thought of an extension to a possible solution. Note everything down in these 5 mins or so.

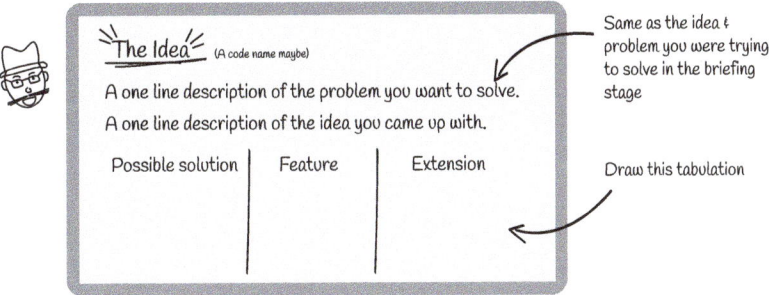

The Idea (A code name maybe)

A one line description of the problem you want to solve.
A one line description of the idea you came up with.

| Possible solution | Feature | Extension |

Same as the idea & problem you were trying to solve in the briefing stage

Draw this tabulation

? Here is what each of the columns mean

Possible solutions: all the solutions which strikes the participants in relation to the main problem statement; an app is not always the final solution.

Features: all the ideas in relation to the creator's idea and possible branches for them.

Extension: if you (the creator) think it's a little difficult to handle in the first version.

Once these "5 or so mins" are completed, let everyone assemble...

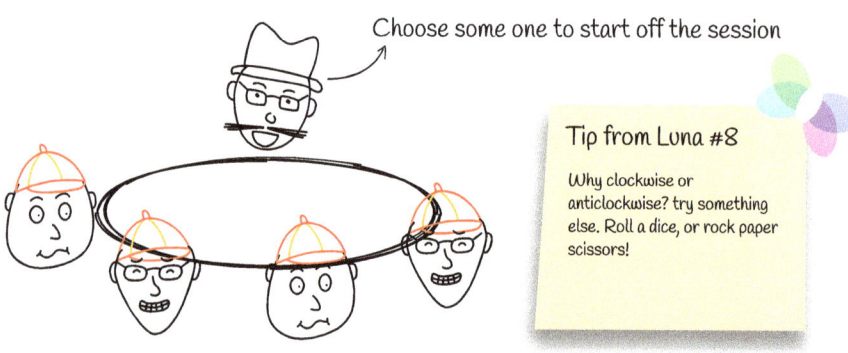

Choose some one to start off the session

Tip from Luna #8

Why clockwise or anticlockwise? try something else. Roll a dice, or rock paper scissors!

 You are now in the excited kids phase no idea is a bad idea.

 But make sure you guys don't go out of bounds by making it too far fetched!

 Now it's triathlon time!

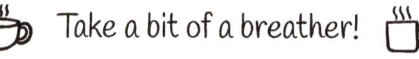 Take a bit of a breather!

Let's ~~cycle~~ fly, swim and Run!

 Stages of Design LUNA

This is the "Air" session

 Tell your solution and the reason behind how you think it would impact the stakeholders and customers.

Tip from Luna #9

Keep it short and simple

 Note down each of the ideas brought up in their respective column. When you are noting down all the ideas being told, make sure you note down only the key words and make them as vague as you can.

> < This is the suspense which will be revealed later > <

After this session is completed, let the participants take a snapshot of all the key points which were noted on the board.

For this session in specific all the participants need to select points from the "idea" tabulation and think for themselves for 5 mins (or however long you want upto 10 mins).

 This is the last session where the partcipants will think in isolation

 From here on... it's a complete group activity

 Once everyone assembles again, repeat the same steps as stated above

 Think outside the box

(Not the first time you are coming across this for sure)

An interesting case study

On how  opened avenues which no one thought before

 The Pontiac Case

I am pretty sure you have come across this case study at some point

If not...

 This is a fun one...

A customer, once entered a Pontiac car service centre stating that his car does not like vanilla flavoured ice-cream!

 The engineers naturally did not understand what the customer was stating...

When asked again, the customer tells the engineers...

 "I go to buy ice-cream from a store near my house and when I buy any flavour other than vanilla my car starts immediately but when I buys vanilla ice-cream my car wont start until I waits for a long time"

Not taking the customers ice cream story serious...
Obviously

The engineers thoroughly inspected the vehicle and told the customer that car was good to go...

Few weeks later....

 The same customer...

With the same vanilla story...

This time after the initial inspection of the vehicle...

One of the engineer wanted to test the "vanilla ice-cream" hypothesis.

 Now off the engineer and the customer were to buy ice-creams...

The engineer first bought a chocolate flavoured ice-cream the car started just fine!

The next day...

He bought a strawberry flavoured ice-cream the car started fine this time as well

The next day he bought the vanilla ice-cream...

 the car did not start...

Not believing the ice-cream was at problem

He did this test couple of times over the course of a few days...
He was presented with the same results...

After observing the ice-cream parlour for a couple of days the engineers figured it out...

The vanilla flavour was so popular that storage for it was near the cash register compared to the other flavours which were much further in the store.

When anyone bought any other flavour it would give the car enough time to cool down!

But when it was vanilla there was no time for the car to cool down!

 A unique insight to look at a problem in various angles and scenarios

The most common method might always not be the means to find the final solution!

Now we are in the "Water" session

 We need to keep the stream in the right way, collect feedback from various sources after each of the "Games"!

In this session, you and your team try to bring lot more structure to the solutions, features and ideas which are proposed.

the "Yes and..." Game

Here you and the participants can latch on to a train of thought by one participant and add more and more until you feel it is concrete enough to be executed!

<Idea by participant> "yes and..." <idea by an other participant>

Sample scenario

Idea: Groceries Delivery application.

Run this phase until you think you and your team have a very concrete understanding of the core idea and the proposed solution.

Great! I hope that was a lot of fun and lots of new ideas were brought to light!

 Make sure you are noting down all the key points only...

As the participants and you come up with new ideas

Remember!

Keep them vague!

> < Enough of the suspense > <

Now to relieve you from the Suspense

Not writing the points in detail allows you to think in a more broader way, as you and your team get a lot more clarity, the same point can be viewed in a different light.

Tip from Luna #10
Follow this method until you and your team think "this is it" for a solution/idea

As stated in the tip. If you and your team think a point is a perfect fit, write it down in as much detail as you think feels fit.

This is where you get to "the Grumpy uncle state"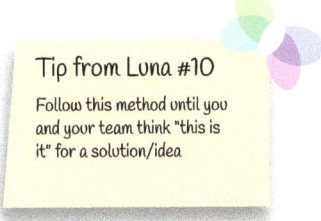

Play the  good cop - bad cop game

This is a fun and interactive way where the participants will be able to identify pitfalls by understanding 2 sides of the problem

Start off with splitting half of the participants in favour of the points raised (Optimist) and the other half of the participants against the points raised (Pessimist).

The participants can switch roles.

Now, the Facilitator reads out the points or a problem in particular. Then the participants can start off by providing points with respective to their side.

Sample scenario

Problem: We need to make our organization more upto date with the latest technology trends.

Congratulations! you found one possible solution

Note this down and share with

This is obviously a sample scenario. In the actual practice, participants do not have to switch side immediately when points are challenged.

Once you have a collection of these points you can get to collecting feedback!

Final phase "the Rock"

Let's make sure your team's solution is rock solid

Incorporate all the changes required to be made from the feedback collected

Now with the updated ideas... let's begin...

 Voting

A tried and tested method but certainly not fool proof.

Participants vote for their favourite idea which were brainstormed in the previous phase.

 The facilitator reads out each of the points and the participants can vote.

Tip from Luna #11

Why just show hand! try something fun why not yell out the idea's name! It would keep the energy high

 Wait! your idea was voted out?!?

Its time to revolt!!!

~~ Or maybe ~~

 Participant can get around a minute or 2 to pitch why their idea is a good fit and their thought process behind it.

Once you have a list of all the ideas that made the cut...

You are good to go...

 ## Luna has an important point to make

 You can only think so much... Mental block is eminent :(

 But, No problem a quick walk cannot solve! or something to change your mind for a bit, that should do the trick.

 Once you are back from your break, gaze around your surrounding and notice objects in the room that could spark a new thought!

Tip from Luna #12

Thinking about the same thing in the same way can hinder your freedom of thought. Try something new to fire those neurons again!

 Also try to look up random images from the internet that could also help you come up with a fresh new idea or solution.

Well, now that you and your team are all setup and have a very good understanding about the idea and the problem it is trying to solve, Let's start off with the fun stuff

 Product brain storming

Notes:

Notes:

Chapter

3ᶜ

Stages of Design LUNA/
Get...Set..GO!

Problem Solutioning

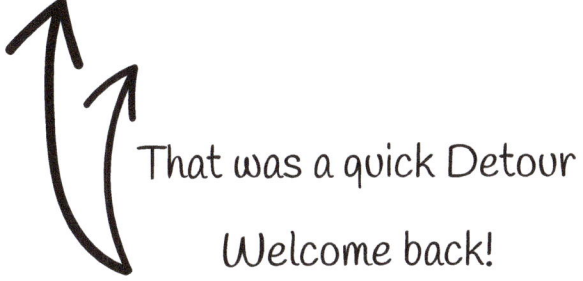

That was a quick Detour

Welcome back!

Let's get to Product brainstorming now

④ Product Brainstorm

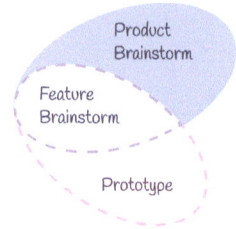

We know how to collect feedback and brainstorm, so now... let's put it to work.

In this stage you will be brainstorming the overall solution.

Once you and your team feel satisfied with the points collected... you guessed it collect feedback!

Start off by brainstorming all the avenues necessary that would help the end customers and stakeholders of the end product.

During this step, you might come across new stakeholders or customer segments to include.

Identify the key stakeholders, customer, customer segments in this phase.

In this phase you are searching for all the

Core identities   USP

That makes *The Idea Name* unique just like you!

Utilize the 3 sessions to ensure the *best* ideas are selected!

Air   Water   Rock

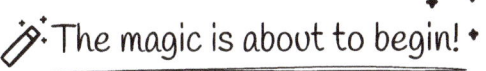

🪄 The magic is about to begin! ✦

The facilitator needs to set the act first before the Magic commences...

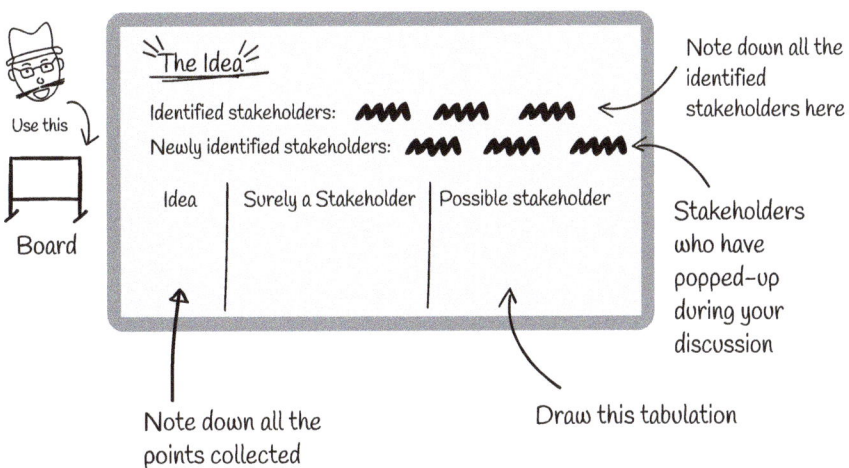

Note down all the identified stakeholders here

Stakeholders who have popped-up during your discussion

Note down all the points collected

Draw this tabulation

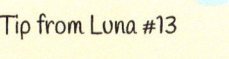 Now that we have our board ready! let's start off!

Start from the first "idea" onwards discuss among yourselves who are the stakeholders that are certainly part of this idea and who could possibly be added.

Tip from Luna #13

Stuck? couldn't come to an agreement? no problem, visit that point again a little later!

 Take about 3 – 4 minutes per idea

✅ Time for some critiquing!

Follow the feedback methods on design LUNA

Get out there and get some feedback!

Once you and your team are back, brainstorm on the new points before going to the next phase

⑤ Feature Brainstorm

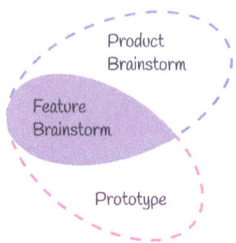

 This is going to be The most fun phase!!

Here you are going to brainstorm on all the possible features you want ☆*The Idea Name*☆ to have.

In this phase you are searching for all the

Features   Relation

That makes ☆*The Idea Name*☆ intuitive and creative like you 😊

Alright, but how do we brainstorm in this phase?

 Throwing your ideas in random and following no order is the name of the game!

Why? cause going one point at a time will become too limiting!

This will ensure... all the ideas you came up with from the "product brainstorm" session will be covered and more importantly you will be able to establish a link between ideas and features!

 Have an idea just speak it out!

There are 3 main steps we need to hop on to complete this phase

First step: Throwing ideas and deciding its importance

Second step: Mapping features and establishing a relation between them

Third step: Prioritizing versioning

A completely different plane step: costing capabilities and bridge to last phase of LUNA

The first step

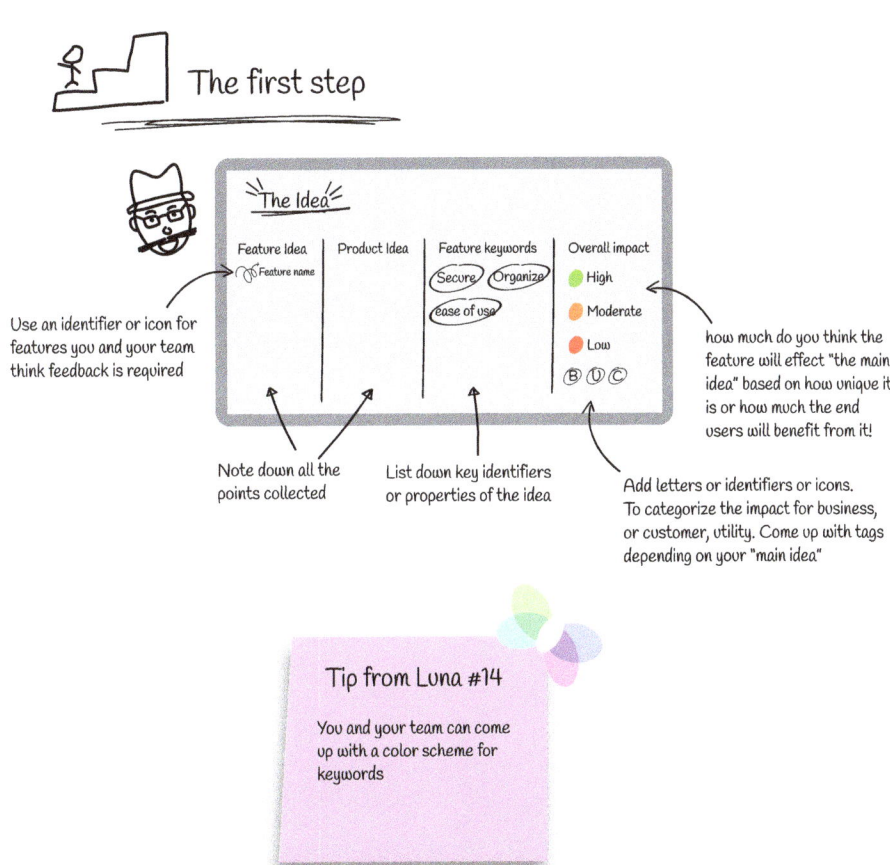

 ## The second step

Well you and your team have certainly come up with some really good ideas!

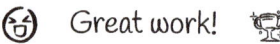 Great work!

Now comes the part where you and your team create a family tree for all the features!

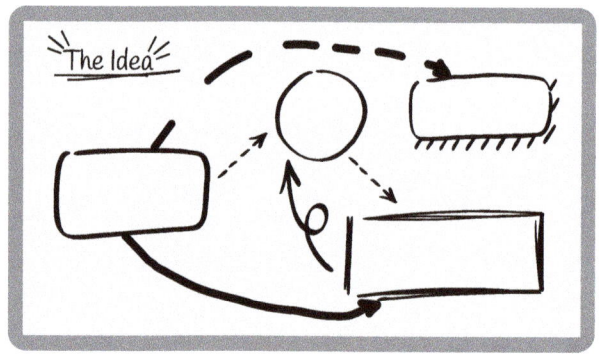

Tip from Luna #15

Use different shapes, arrow and line styles instead of only one style! it would be easy to read and understand later!

 2 Up one last to go!

"The third step" is the last mandatory step in our 3+1 step process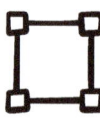

The Third step

Phew! that second step took too long didn't it?

This step wont take as long... Promise!

Now let's prioritize and version the features you and your team have come up with.

From the previous step, you and your team might have identified which of the features are "main features" and "sub features" that are dependent on these "main features".

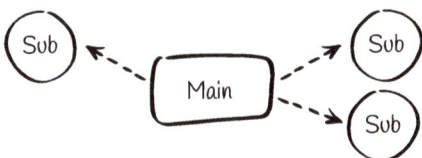

🚩 This table will define the way you and your team are planning to release features once the actual work starts...

Tip from Luna #16
Prioritize features in a way where all the highly prioritized ones make it to your first release. Lower prior are the ones which will be added in later versions.

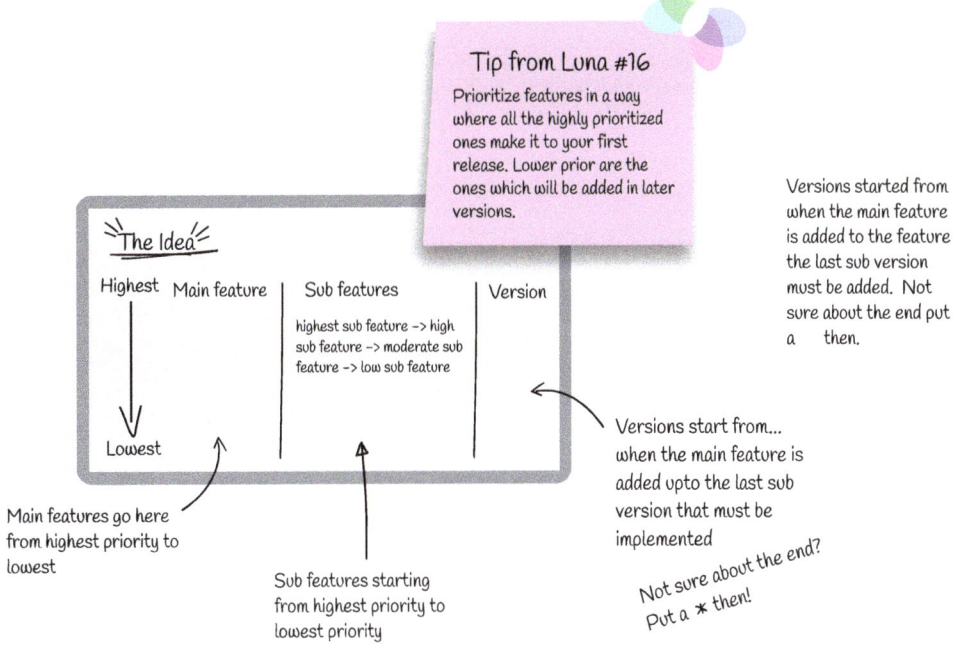

Versions started from when the main feature is added to the feature the last sub version must be added. Not sure about the end put a ✱ then.

The Idea

Highest — Main feature | Sub features | Version

highest sub feature -> high sub feature -> moderate sub feature -> low sub feature

Lowest

Main features go here from highest priority to lowest

Sub features starting from highest priority to lowest priority

Versions start from... when the main feature is added upto the last sub version that must be implemented

Not sure about the end? Put a ✱ then!

"The completely different plane" step

Well how did that go? all your features versioned and ready to go?

Now, let's see how well are you geared up for starting off!

Tip from Luna #17

If a sub feature requires special attention, note them down in the features section

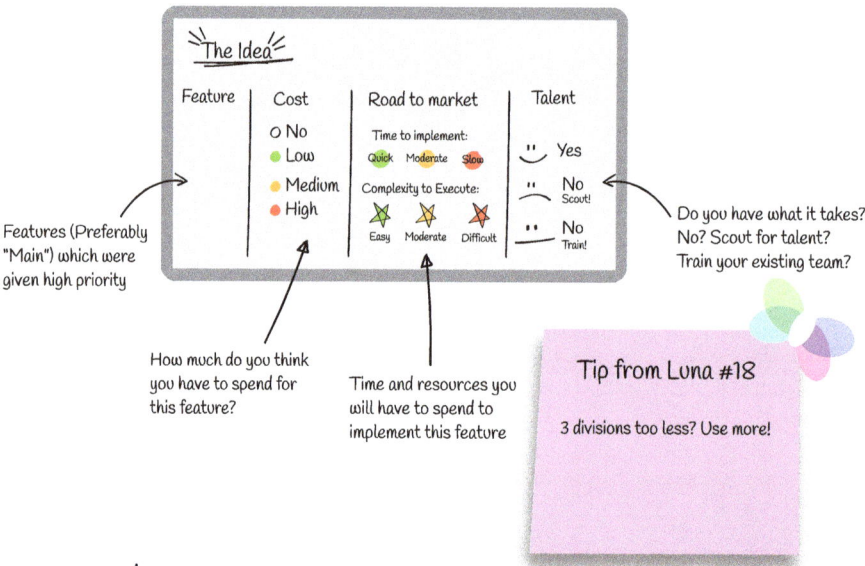

Features (Preferably "Main") which were given high priority

How much do you think you have to spend for this feature?

Time and resources you will have to spend to implement this feature

Do you have what it takes? No? Scout for talent? Train your existing team?

Tip from Luna #18

3 divisions too less? Use more!

 Now we are done with the astral aspects as well!

Time to get to work!

Round up the teams... Now its time to create the prototype masterpiece!

⑥ Prototyping

 Ahh, our journey is nearing the end!
This is the final stage of LUNA!

 Feedback is the most important aspect once you have completed creating your prototype

 By the way! Prototyping is creating "The Idea"'s blueprint, both for you and your customer.

We will be identifying the talent which is required, avenues to generate revenue, Customers you will have to onboard and more...

There are 2 main journeys we need to embark in "Prototyping"

Business Strategy Flow   Customer Journey

This will help make *The Idea Name* more efficient and crystal clear once you and your team get to work!

Business Strategy Flow

In business strategy flow, our goal is to understand and identify the core components to bring the idea to life!

Note down all possible avenues for (each block)

Here is what we have to do!

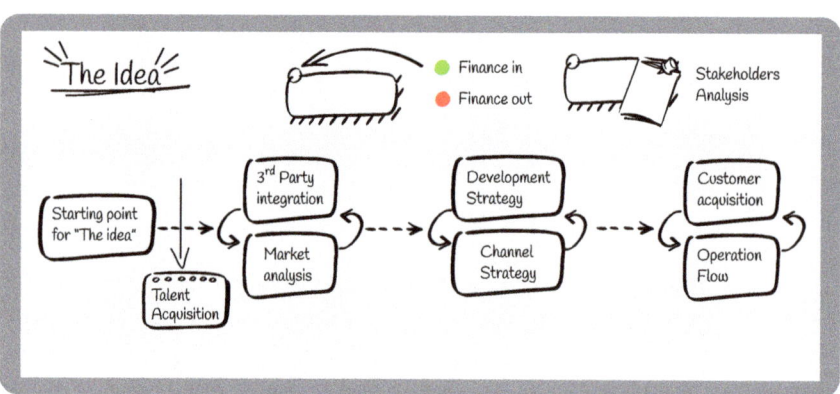

 Correlated Steps
Steps happen in parallel, but change each of the steps based on the decisions made from the other!

These correlated steps will have an impact in the forthcoming steps

⊗

Don't skip any of the blocks until you are completely sure it does not align with your "Idea"

Now let's understand (the block) using our grocery delivery app!

Starting point

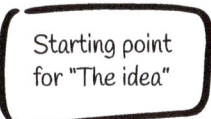

The initial point where your customer will start using your "idea"

There can be many starting points for your idea like:
1. App
2. Website
3. Physical store
4. A physical devices
5. Authorized Personnel

Ask yourself

"From where can my customers interact with my idea?"

 In our case an application for customers, delivery personnel, and a web dashboard for store owners.

 Match your path!

Find out who your customers are, and figure out how they interact with your Idea!

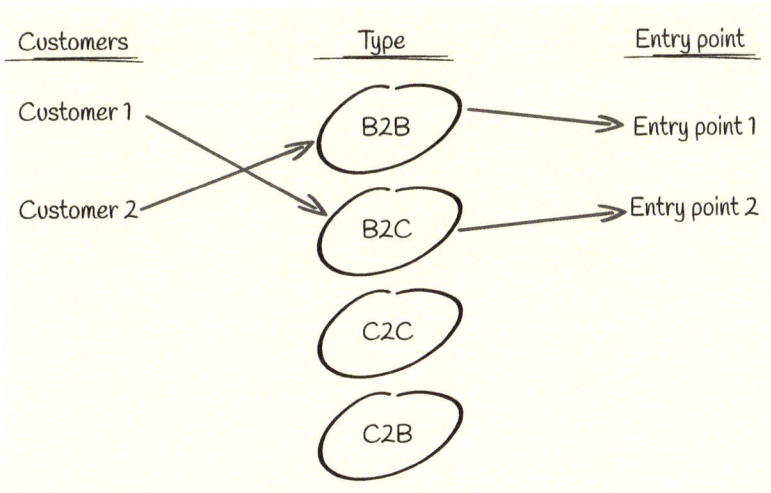

While doing this activity, you and your team might stumble upon possible hybrid models like B2B2C

Talent Acquisition

How you are planning to acquire the talent required for the idea?

You have already collected this in the previous step.

 Now you need to figure out the avenues to find them.

How are you going to recruit the right people for the job? speak with known connects. Find companies which provide people with required skill sets.

Ask yourself

"What are the immediate avenues to get the people I am looking for?"

- Post add on freelancing portals for UI/UX designers.
- Get CVs from recruitment portals.
- Speak with locals to help with delivery at the start.

Tip from Luna #19

Too complicated? No problem, The next step will surely help out!

In this step you need to fill this list:

Identified role which is required for your business model
_____

3 point talent description
1. _____
2. _____
3. _____

How are you planning to acquire this talent

Write your actions here

3rd Party integration

External parties that need to be involved. It could be people or software or a service

Anything that could tie your idea and the stakeholder together for a seamless business flow.

Ask yourself

"Could I link anything with my idea instead of doing it from scratch?"

- Tying up with a company that helps with delivery.
- Maps for Users and Delivery personnel
- Email and Phone services
- OTP generation

Before we get to the questionnaire, you and your team need to...

List all the third party integrations with your "Idea"

What are you integrating for?   Which category does it fall under:
☑ Product ☑ Service ○ People

 For each integration fill this

The 3rd party identification Questionnaire

Who are all the vendors you identified

What are the key services you need from them

What value they can add to your product

What should be the cost to service ratio

How best should they be at their service

Market analysis

This is going to be a long one!

Make sure you are ready for the ride!

✓ So... these are the list of questions you will have to ask among yourselves.

Let's make this a lot more interactive... shall we?

Match all the possible 👓 with 👏

10/10 We already completed one for you. Now you and your team can finish the rest!

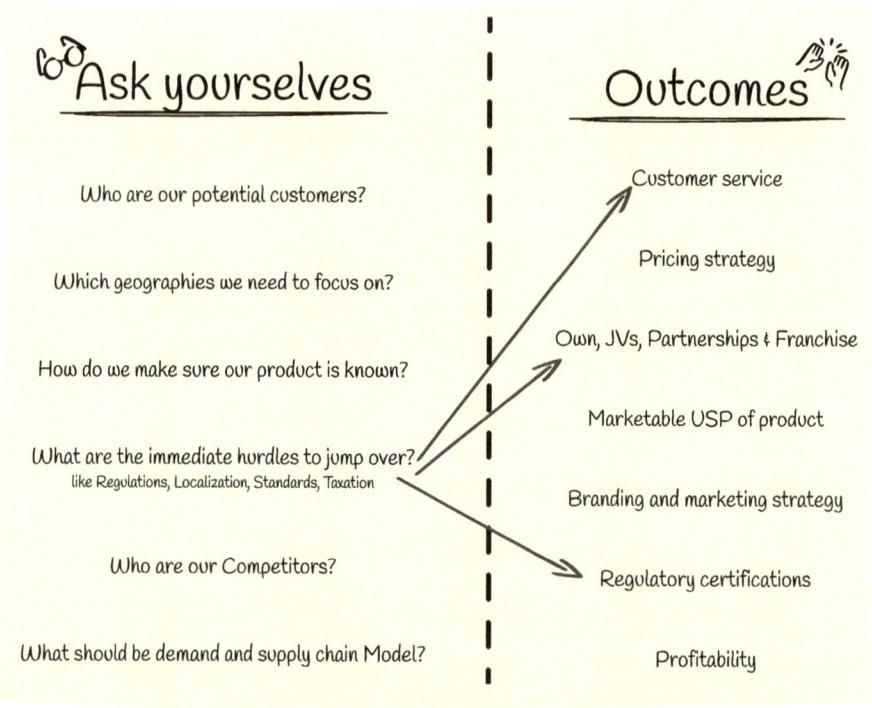

👓 Ask yourselves

- Who are our potential customers?
- Which geographies we need to focus on?
- How do we make sure our product is known?
- What are the immediate hurdles to jump over? like Regulations, Localization, Standards, Taxation
- Who are our Competitors?
- What should be demand and supply chain Model?

👏 Outcomes

- Customer service
- Pricing strategy
- Own, JVs, Partnerships & Franchise
- Marketable USP of product
- Branding and marketing strategy
- Regulatory certifications
- Profitability

Development Strategy

Development Strategy

Your idea is here to make everyone happy.

🎯 Focus on these keywords to delight the below stakeholders:

Customers
- Innovative
- Social Status
- Service
- Price
- User friendly
- Quality

Suppliers
- Branding
- Efficiency
- Service
- Profitability
- Network effect
- Quality
- Customer base

Employees
- Innovation
- Social Status
- Productivity
- Benefits
- Work Culture
- Growth

Shareholders
- Innovative
- Governance
- Growth
- Revenue
- Transformation
- Score card

📚 This step will help you and your team define KPIs

Ask yourself 👓

"What would I do if I was in their shoes?"

- Ensuring delivery personnel safety
- Rewards for loyal and frequent customers
- Bonus rewards for timely delivery

Channel Strategy

How does your idea flow before reaching the customer?

Taking the data collected from the "Market analysis" step.
We need to build a strategy to make it happen!

Here is what you will need to identify

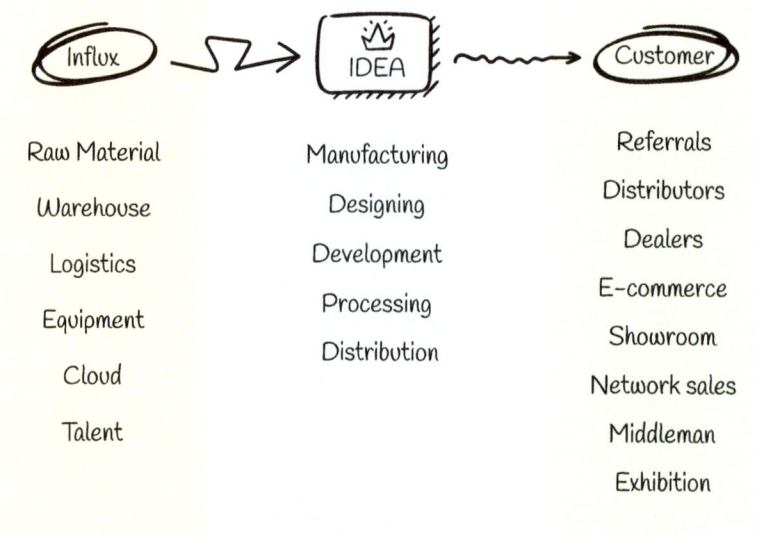

Influx	IDEA	Customer
Raw Material	Manufacturing	Referrals
Warehouse	Designing	Distributors
Logistics	Development	Dealers
Equipment	Processing	E-commerce
Cloud	Distribution	Showroom
Talent		Network sales
		Middleman
		Exhibition

Ask yourself

Influx ⟿ "How are we going to source materials?"
IDEA ⟶ "How can I effectively utilize what I have obtained from 'influx'?"
Customer ⟵ "How do my potential customers experience my Idea?"

- Tie up with shops for groceries and other items (Raw materials)
- Ensure settlement between customer and stores (Processing)
- Distribute orders evenly across delivery personnel (Distribution)
- I will place standees near store I have tied up with (Exhibition)

Customer Acquisition

People love your IDEA!

Great Job! Now its time to make them your customer!

Categorize your potential customers into:

Loyal to you | Ready to switch | Ready to try | Loyal to competitor

Using these faces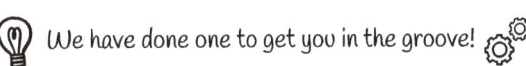

For each of the approaches below, choose all possible customer types.

We have done one to get you in the groove!

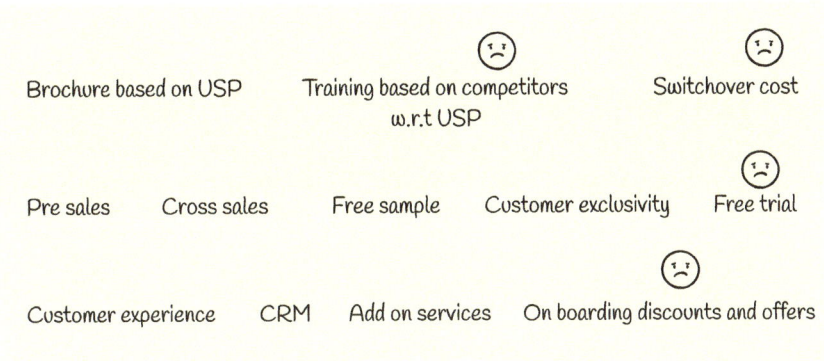

Brochure based on USP | Training based on competitors w.r.t USP 🙁 | Switchover cost 🙁

Pre sales | Cross sales | Free sample | Customer exclusivity | Free trial 🙁

Customer experience | CRM | Add on services | On boarding discounts and offers 🙁

Ask yourself

"Why would someone want to use my Idea?"

- Gift hamper on birthdays - Loyal customers
- free delivery for first 2 orders - Ready to switch
- Refined app layout and experience - Ready to try
- Setup flea market to try app - Loyal to competitor

Operation Flow

 How are your going to make sure your Idea flows smoothly.

You and your team will be looking at possible avenues which indirectly effect the main functioning of your idea.

Required ⟹ Stuff required to kick start your idea
Mandatory ⟹ Stuff required by law for your idea

	At the start	After a while
Required	Indirect Procurement	Finance
	Intellectual property filling	Customer care
		Org struct.
	Data privacy	
		Taxes
	Legal	
	Investment	HR
		Terms & conditions
	Refund policy	Regulatory Certifications
		Mandatory

Ask yourself

"How important is this step at the current moment?"

- Food authority certification – Regulatory certification
- Emphasis on delivery policy and safety measures – Terms & conditions
- Deliver goods with company branded eco bags – Indirect procurement

Customer Journey

In Customer Journey, our objective is to identify customers and define various steps involved in experiencing "the idea".

Note down all possible avenues for (each block)

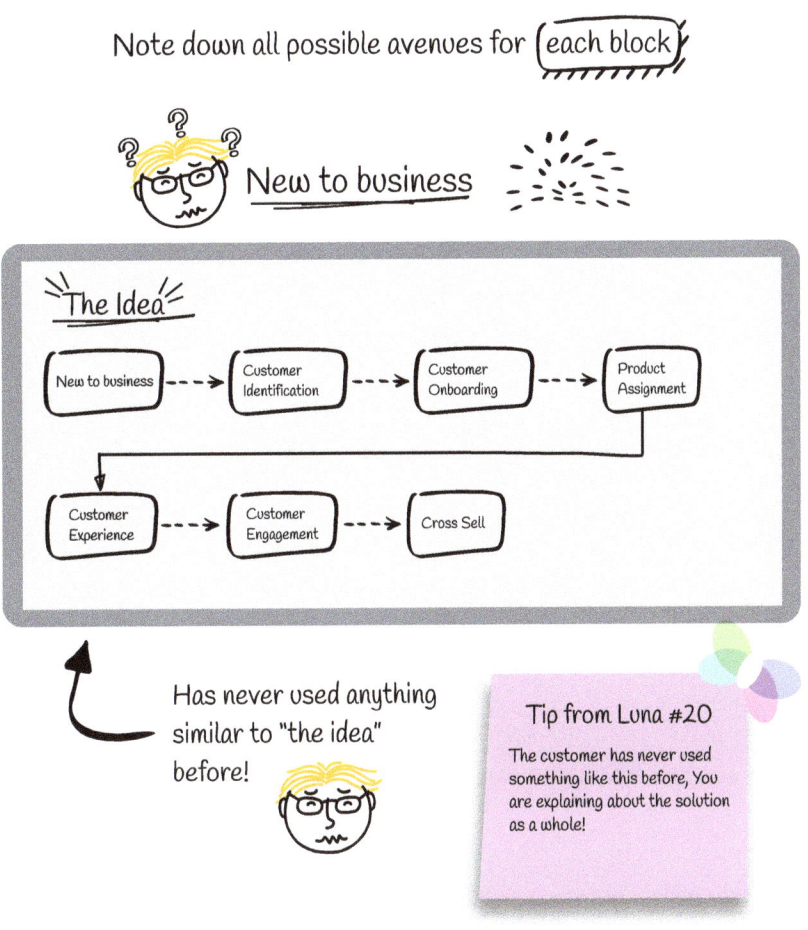

Has never used anything similar to "the idea" before!

Tip from Luna #20

The customer has never used something like this before, You are explaining about the solution as a whole!

You will spend more time in explaining why a person needs to use this solution!

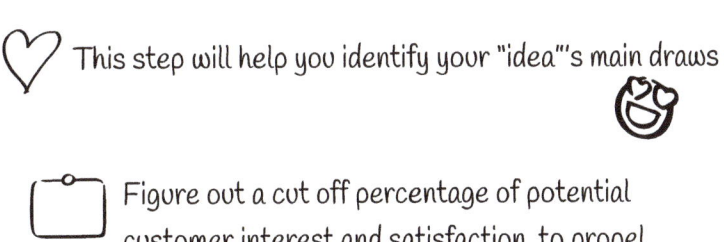

♡ This step will help you identify your "idea"'s main draws

▢ Figure out a cut off percentage of potential customer interest and satisfaction, to propel you to make it happen!

Stages of Design LUNA

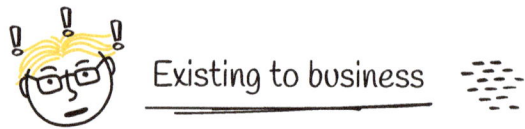
Existing to business

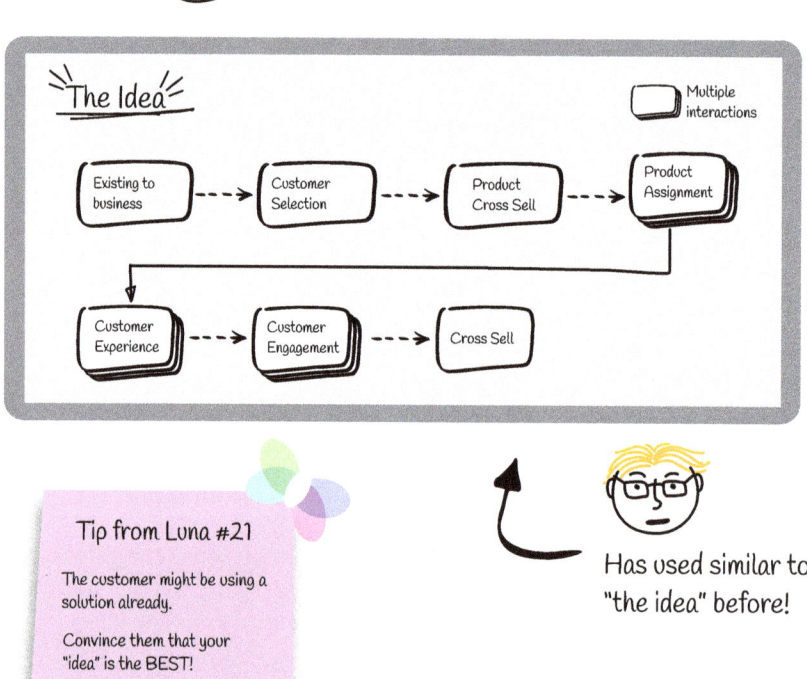

Tip from Luna #21

The customer might be using a solution already.

Convince them that your "idea" is the BEST!

Has used similar to "the idea" before!

You will spend more time in explaining why a person needs to use YOUR solution!

 This step will help you identify your "idea"'s marketable USP

Describe your potential customer's switch over cost. Decisions to be taken to spend more in marketing or rewarding customers or no stress!

Stages of Design LUNA

Outcomes

Ask yourselves

Stages of Design LUNA

Outcomes

Ask yourselves

Stages of Design LUNA

What are you integrating for?

Which category does it fall under:

○ Product   ○ Service   ○ People

Which category does it fall under:

○ Product   ○ Service   ○ People

What are you integrating for?

Notes:

Notes:

Notes:

Notes:

Now, its time to Fly!

 Well, our journey has officially come to an end.

☺ Certainly your ideas are more concrete than ever before.

 Hopefully you and your team had a blast in participating in all the activities!

You can now feel the balance around the idea.

↻ A quick peek into the past

We started off by identifying our "How"s

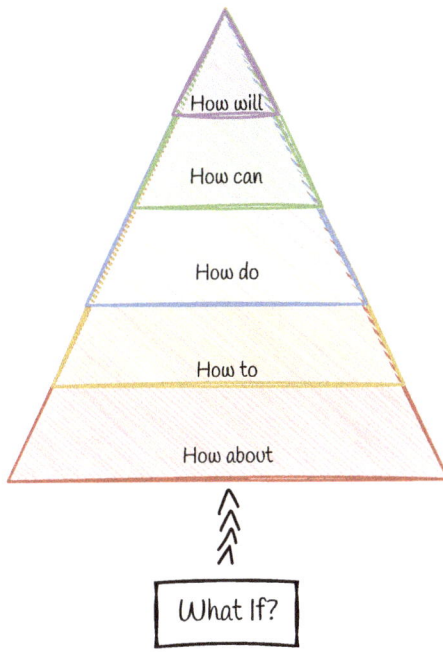

Then we met someone special

Problem Statement

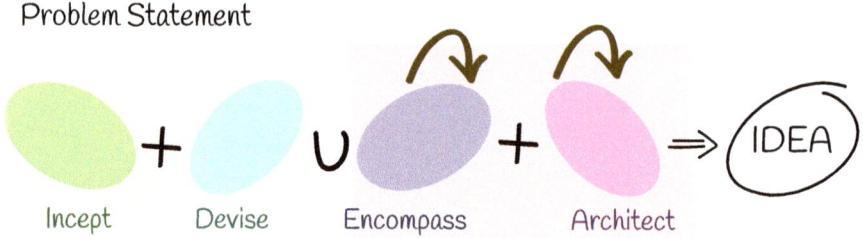

Problem Solutioning

Then we spent most of our time in the 6 stages of Design LUNA

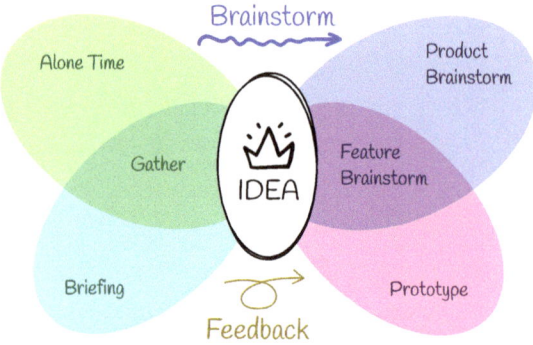

We have also gone through:

Which further improved the IDEA!

For each of the phase you have gone through, a different transformation but these remain common...

Think → Assemble → Communicate → Develop

One last task list

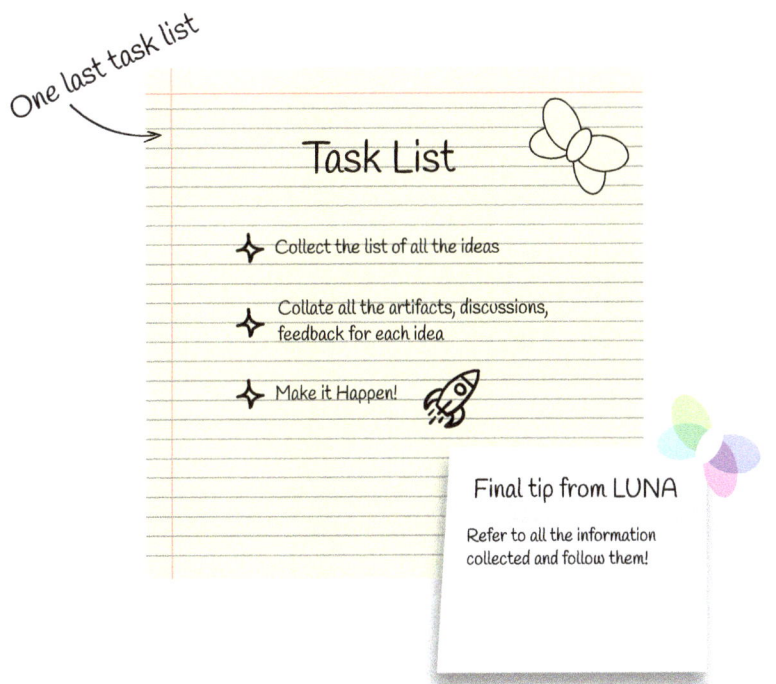

Task List

- Collect the list of all the ideas
- Collate all the artifacts, discussions, feedback for each idea
- Make it Happen!

Final tip from LUNA

Refer to all the information collected and follow them!

Yay! You and your team have now completed Thinking the LUNA way!

My key takeaways:

Reflect with LUNA

How would you rate yourself in these categories

Alone Time

Gather

Briefing

Product Brainstorm

Feature Brainstorm

Prototype

Brainstorm

Feedback

Reflect with LUNA

How would you rate yourself in these categories

Alone Time

Gather

Briefing

Product Brainstorm

Feature Brainstorm

Prototype

Brainstorm

Feedback

Stages of Design LUNA

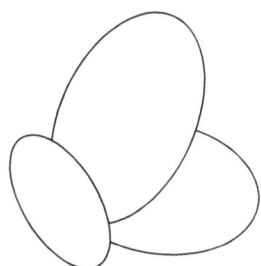

✂ Keep track of important topics...Make your LUNA book Marks

Chapter

4

Cool as ICE

Seems like you are hooked!

Great! here are some fun things you can try out as you start off with your Idea journey!

Who are you thinking of...?

Let's find out who are the core people that would be part of your "Idea"!

First note down your "Idea"'s core or key characteristic

Now let's get the names flowing...

Step 1: All the people you thought of...

All the names that came to your mind, write them down outside the circle

Step 2: Select people to add inside the circle...

These are the people you are confident that they will take the idea to the next level!

Cool as ICE

Characteristic: _____

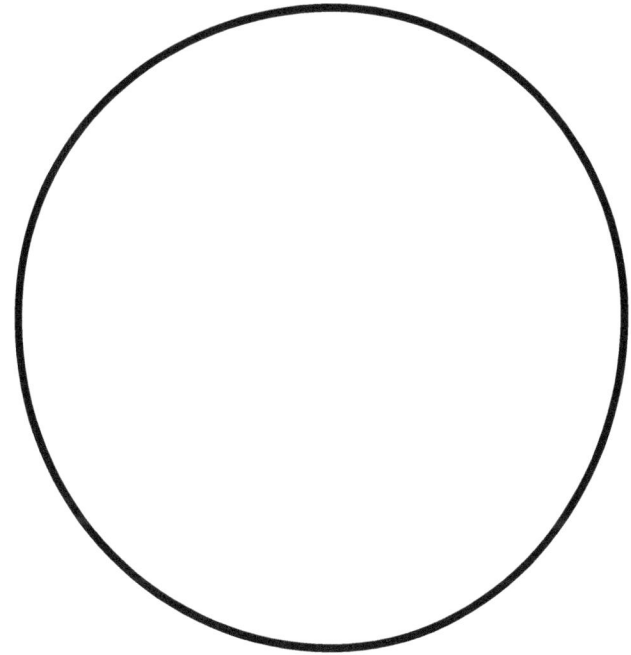

✂ Share this with your team!

Understand your team "Experience" wise

Here is a fun little activity you and your team can take part in!

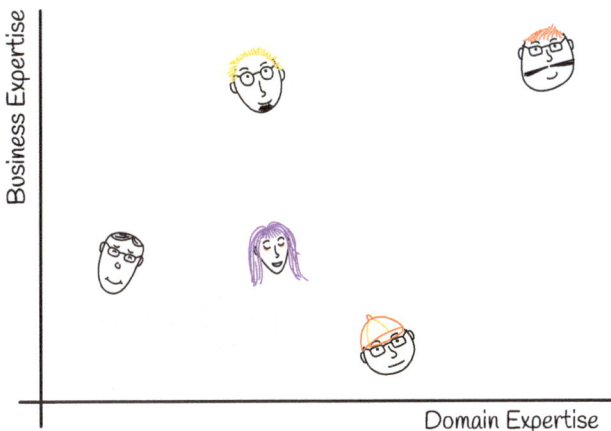

Note down your team member's name in their corresponding quadrant position!

Cool as ICE

Share this with your team! ✂

Domain Expertise

Business Expertise

Identify each members idea language!

⇒ Do you spontaneously come up with an idea?

⇒ Do you like to compile ideas and figure out how to make them better?

Everyone's style plays a pivotal role in making the idea come to life!

Here is an example:

Mukundh Bhushan   :

Cool as ICE

Fill the names of your team members:

_____ : 🔥 🌪

_____ : 🔥 🌪

_____ : 🔥 🌪

_____ : 🔥 🌪

_____ : 🔥 🌪

_____ : 🔥 🌪

_____ : 🔥 🌪

_____ : 🔥 🌪

_____ : 🔥 🌪

_____ : 🔥 🌪

Understand your Product's life cycle better...
Here is a fun little activity you and your team can take part in!

Fills the names who will be heading the following:

Product Initiator: _____
- The person who got the idea

Product Owner: _____
- The person who is going to head the implementation of "the idea"

Product Marketer: _____
- The person who is coming up with a marketing strategy along with their team

Product Operator: _____
- The person who is going to look after things like subscription, lead conversions, customer enquiries, etc

Now let's engage these teams!

Quick legend:

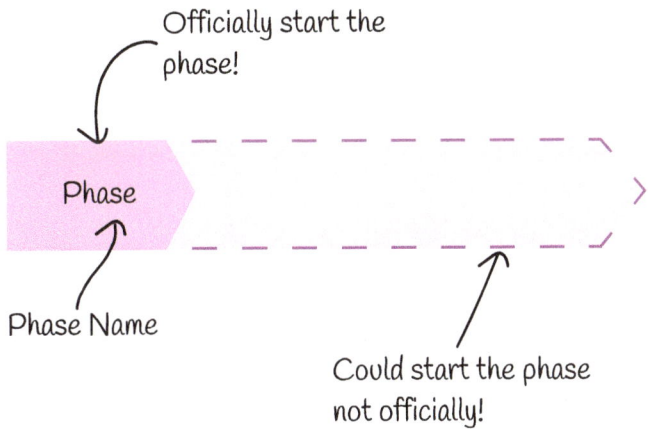

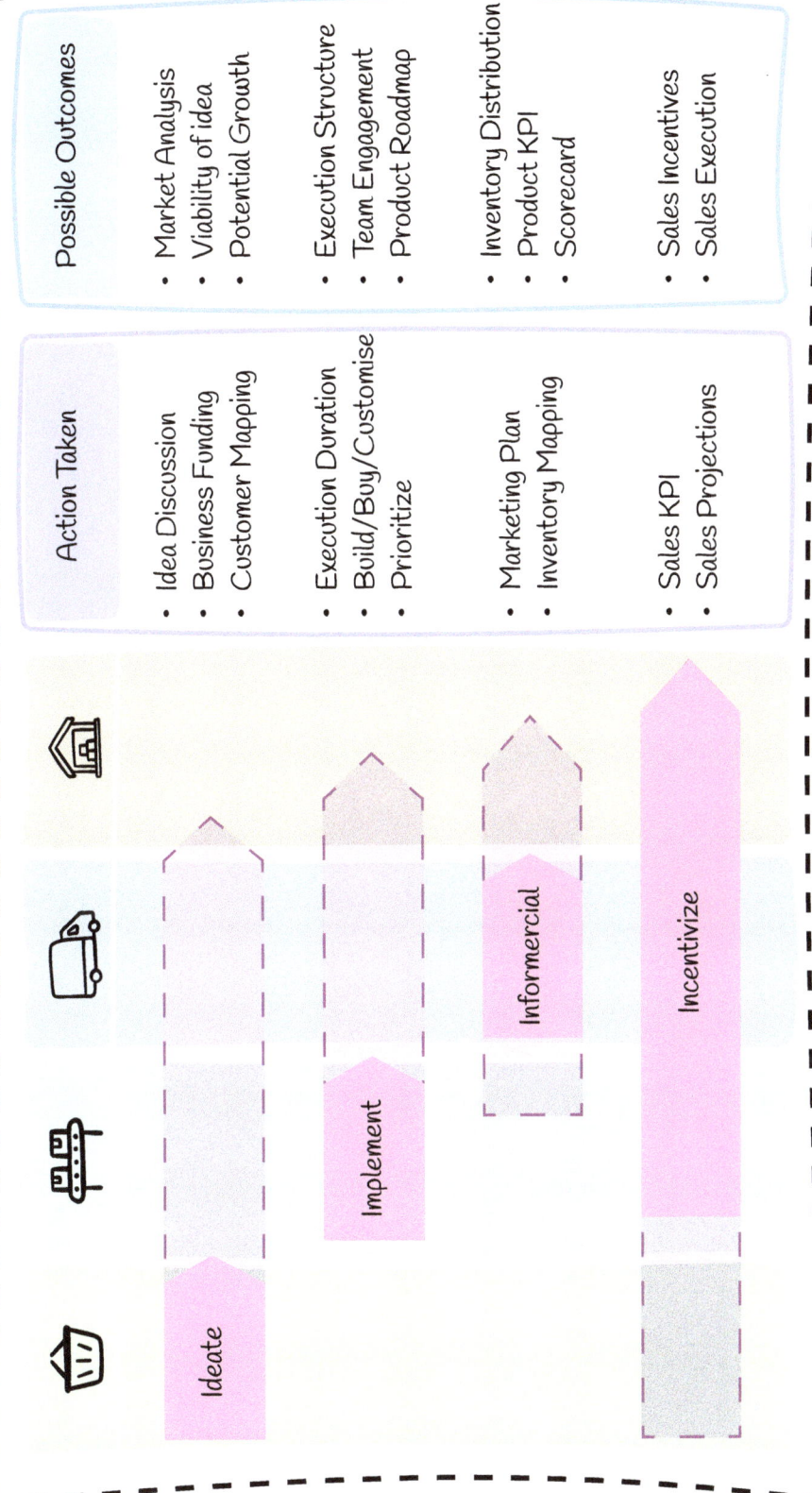

 Oh! You are still here!

You are in for a treat!

From LOST to Design LUNA

So many amazing Expeditions we have embarked along with LUNA...

Here are few "Expeditions" with varying requirements, stakeholders, backgrounds and most importantly varying Ideas!

Here is the plan for the expeditions we will be covering!

- No LUNA?!?
- More Communication!
- Prototyping!
- Feedback!

Through these expeditions you can get an insight on how we were able to design... Design LUNA.

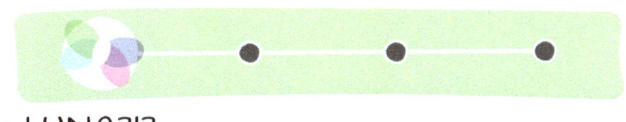

No LUNA?!?

Expedition #1

Greyffiti

www.greyffiti.com

Yay our first expedition together!

Let's get our LUNA checklist set up

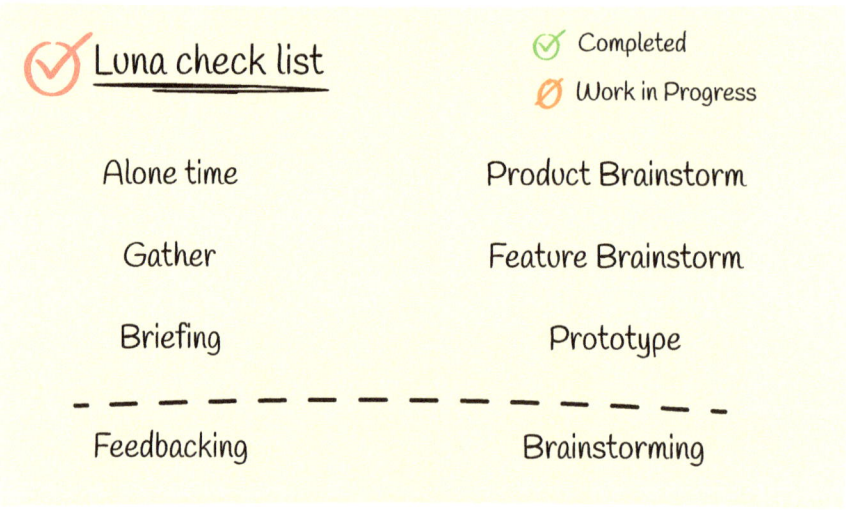

Nothing checked yet, let's see how many we check off with this product!

Greyffiti our first ever product which we designed and developed!

Background

When we first started out our company, I being the founder REALLY wanted to make video games!

Computer gaming was how I was introduced to computers and also computer programming!

So... naturally starting a company which designs and develops games was my dream!

⚡ Immediate problems

Well, all I knew about games was from playing them and developing few mini games using the "unity game engine".

👑 Nothing too fancy for releasing one. ⊗

I did know 3D modelers, developers and sound engines were required, but had no clue about character designers, level designers, game testers and the plethora of people required to create a game!

🎯 Well worth a shot!

So, I started off by finding 3D modellers first.

The idea was... once work with the 3D modeller starts, I could hunt for developers in parallel.

After a bit of hunting I found a 3D animation company who could help me out.

 Great!

Now, my game could be a reality!

Now its time to catch hold of developers for the game, we set out on that mission.

🚢 As our developer hunt was underway... We got the first render of our main character!

Even though we had to work a lot on the detailing and had wanted to change few elements of the characters appearance...

We were more than 'excited!'

Now, we wanted to use this first rendered character as a way to find our developers!

By asking them to make it perform few actions like moving around, jumping etc. using user inputs.

An Important road block

So the characters were sent to me in an email as an image like jpegs or pngs...

[JPG] so no big deal. 👍

But, the developers need to use the actual 3D file so we sent it through an email...

⏰ After a couple of hours... ⏰

We receive an email from the developer, that a few shader files and a couple of other files were missing in the earlier email.

So we zipped the entire folder and tried sharing it with the developer.

And now... the attachment size exceeded the allowed limit.

😟 Great! so cloud drive it is I guess... ☁️

We tried some of the cloud drives out there but each of them had different limitations thus, we were not able to upload and share the character 3D model.

So now the 3D modeler started sending a group files as an email.

Took too long... And now a new problem

A minor change in the file? not an issue we can spend another eternity grouping and send them!

My LUNA moment!

This seemed like an amazing product IDEA, where creators can share their files and folders with a larger storage limits and also track and revert back changes at will. This was the base IDEA.

Alone time added to LUNA?

Not quite... this was the first "Alone time" before "Design LUNA" was even a thing for us yet!

I spent a good day thinking what we can do, what features could be added and most importantly role-playing as the:

① 3D modeler
② The person who knows what's going on
③ The person who does not quite understand what is going on

This alone time was immensely useful... as from the small IDEA which I got, I was able to add a bunch of more features as well!

A slight change in course

 This IDEA was my next big thing!

This could massively help and boost the productivity of my team and also for my customers when it was ready!

🔑 I started to now figure out a team needed for this billion dollar idea! ✳️

Stuck in my own world!

My first plan of action was to get an UI/UX designer.

Where we can sketch out:

- ✓ Application flow
- ✓ Figure out journeys
- ✓ Wire frames

☆ Most importantly see, if, in the due course of designing this product... we could add more features.

? Here is where things did not quite make sense to me. ?

Because, whoever I spoke to started sketching out cloud storage type solutions.

 Which it was not!

Stories make the connections

Well something was missing... why was everyone coming up with a similar approach even though it was not!

After looking back and realizing that I just told them the product and not a lot else. This is the problem mostly.

After the previous "minor" setback, I went back to the UI/UX designer, who I felt was able to understand the product to a certain extent.

Even though, I did "a not so good" job in telling them why it is that I am building greyffiti! the last time.

💭 This time it needs to be different... 💭

So this time I built a story on why I am making this tool and also how it could possibly improve their UI/UX workflow!

A connection in a lost island!

✧ This worked wonders! ✧

The designer was immediately able to connect with the idea! and now was able to understand the scope of it much better.

There was a lot more energy when we communicated!

The questions raised this time were a lot more relevant and something we both could discuss about!

Through our interactions, we were able to add lot more features!

"Interactions"? Do you mean brainstorming?

No, not really cause there was no structure in place yet.

But...

It was through this "iterations"... while we were throwing ideas that we figured out the

"Yes and..." method!

So what next for this IDEA

Well the usual, finding developers for frontend and backend development.

Once we found the right set of people, we just started off with the development.

Hmm... that's it?
Of course not, they have a bigger impact in our next expedition!

Let's check the checklist again!

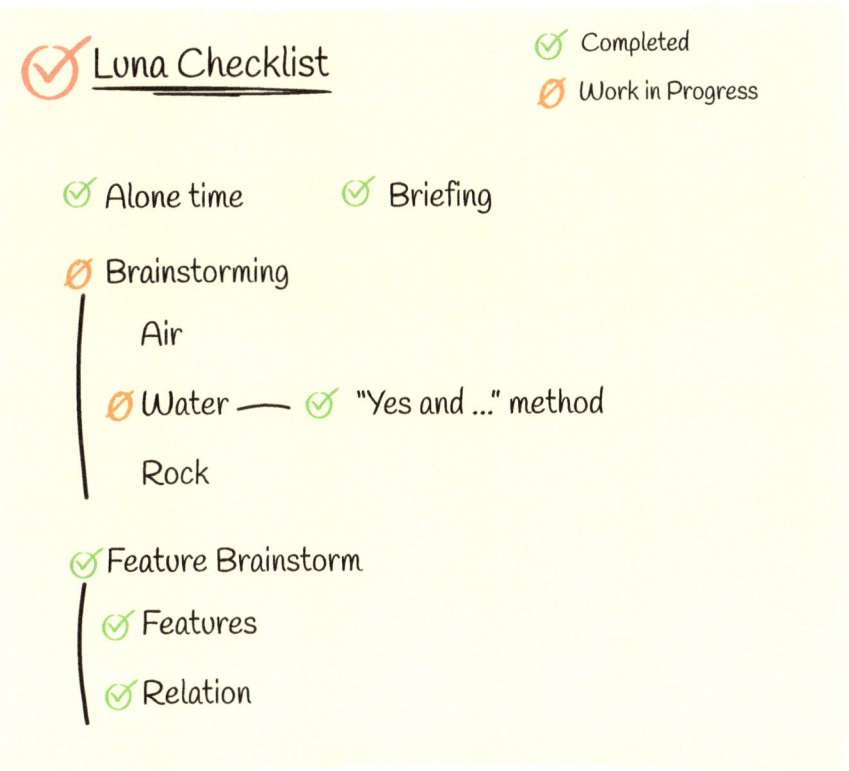

More Communication!

Expedition #2

FEDDUP

www.feddup.me

OK! great to see you again!

Let's see how we are doing so far in our checklist!

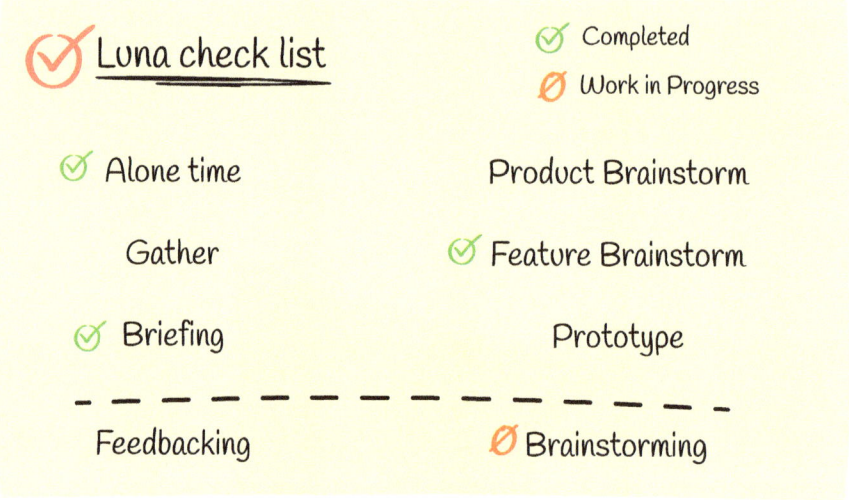

 Seems like we did find a couple of points with our first expedition! Now for more!

Let's get started!

Almost Background

After we jumped over all the hurdles we developed the alpha version of Greyffiti!

Now it was time for us to start the closed user group testing!

We shared it with the 3D modelling company, who were helping us out with our game, a few companies and freelancers which were in creation space.

Different companies, Different teams, all of them creators!

Back to school with

A new tool that no one has used before...

not very obvious right at the get go!

So... We had to train people who would be using it and later on provide their feedback!

Immediate problem

After about a week of them playing around with greyffiti

Wait a week... so kind of immediate...

Anyways... We started getting heaps of emails regarding:

- 🐞 Bugs they had encountered,
- ❓ Stuff which not working as they thought it would.
- 😐 Confusing placements of some elements
- ♡ Most importantly, very useful and interesting suggestions which could greatly help greyffiti.

Now the problem was we were getting so many emails and messages that sorting and prioritizing them became a nightmare for me and my team.

Some of the feedback or suggestions we received were similar to each other...

Some of which we had to revert back and clarify what exactly the issue was...

Some who wanted tweaking in parameters for better functioning.

    ...and more and more and more!

🚫 Too many points... too little patience

So... we did have time, but we were kind of lazy to do the same thing again and again...

Anyways, pushing through the laziness and overwhelming feeling of looking at the number of points we had to sort and filter out.

Firstly, we told the companies and freelancers to please halt for a few days!

    ⚙️ Now to sorting and filtering!

We sat for a couple of days and got them all arranged and prioritized.

    Great! That was a lot of work!

    🖥️ Now to development >_

2 way Communication

Once a batch of bugs were fixed or some of the provided suggestions were added to the tool...

We sent out emails and messages to make sure everyone is upto date with everything new on greyffiti.

And we started checking off each of the points which we have completed and tested

But now the issue was the users so the companies and freelancers were finding it difficult to keep track of all the email that we were sending.

    Great! now its a problem on both ends!

We did not want to sort out the emails

    ~~AND~~

They did not want to keep searching and referring to them!

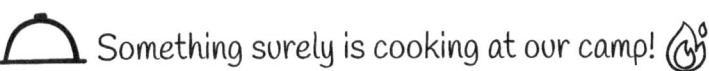

Another LUNA moment!?

In the making for sure! But we still had to figure out what has to be done!

> Time to assemble again... I guess!

We had another problem in hand and something which we knew we had to fix.

A good start for another billion dollar idea... I suppose!

We decided to take a day off and figure out a solution individually.

The Gather phase in full effect!?

The day later rolled by and when we met up again to discuss the solutions.

A team filled with people from different background, experiences and understanding...

That was clearly reflected once we started sharing our potential solutions.

Everyone of us had a different way to look at the exact same problem!

> Sounds like air to me!

The Storm approaches

We were now officially in our Brainstorming phase!

We were throwing ideas around, noting them down and also using the "Yes and ..." method to figure out a lot more ideas.

We were sailing smoothly through these rough waters and making good progress!

 Oops! spoke too soon

But it is a storm after all! two of my team members got into a disagreement, we are enthusiastic people so no hard feelings.

In the due course of this debate, one of my team member told "Be in my shoes for a second and think about it".

My parallel LUNA moment as this was an amazing way to figure out the pitfalls from everone's perspective.

The "Good cop, bad cop" game was shaping up...

We figured out how to add this into our brainstorm process and also our generic workflow.

This greatly helped us to understand ideas in a wider perspective!

So now what?

To start off... we were able to gain a lot of insight over the debate earlier.

And were also able to explore lot more avenues through it.

We, of course added the "Good cop, Bad cop" method to our brainstorming process.

Rock solid yet?

Once we ran our "still under development" brainstorming sessions a couple more times.

We had plenty of ideas, now for everyone's favorite

 "Voting"

So technically... Voting was also added to our brainstorming process... I guess...

Did we start off with this project?

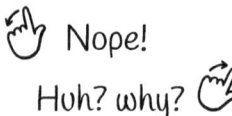 Nope!
Huh? why?

We were about to when something really special happend!

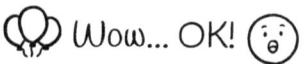 Wow... OK!

I got into a disagreement with someone regarding my latest and greatest idea!

❓ Hmm... how is this special you ask?

This was the un-biased group feedback phase.

For us, our ideas are great because we understand the full extent of its usability and potential!

Well unfortunately, a person no way related to your idea will be able to appreciate it until, you understand their view points as well.

I am still a bit immature, so during this discord, I was not able to identify the gold mine I came across.

It was only after I met up with my team the next day and told them about this interaction and the confusions this person had with feddup.

✨ That we realized the amazing place we were in! ✨

So looks like we are miner now!

Let's see how that turned out! ⛏

Mining underway

...*before we start developing*

We categorized ourselves as the "Biased" crowd...

And we thought it would be a good idea if each of us could strike a similar dialogue with an unbiased crowd.

⊗
   Minus the debate and high emotions of course!

Now... off we were in vaguely explaining Feddup to our unbiased crowd like our parents or siblings or close friends to figure out where people were missing the connection.

 The amount of information we got was Treasure.

Well... we were speaking with well-known people...

So, as you may have guessed... the conversations were not one way anymore, they were more like a dialogue!

And guess what... "What If" questions everywhere!

Once, we were all done with asking our set of people, we got back and started reviewing what we collected.

We, being the biased crowd or more precisely, the team which built the core idea, we were able to figure out solutions and counter arguments to the points raised.

It was only after we gave a closer look to the way we were communicating, that we figured out...

 ....you guess it...

"Why not" everywhere!

The answers to the "what if" questions that we collected were followed by a "why not" answer from us!

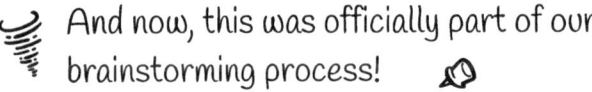

And thus, this is the tale of feddup and how our laziness basically shaped almost the entire feedbacking in Design LUNA!

Now time for our checklist

Phew! that was a long one!

That only mean we get to tick off more from the checklist!

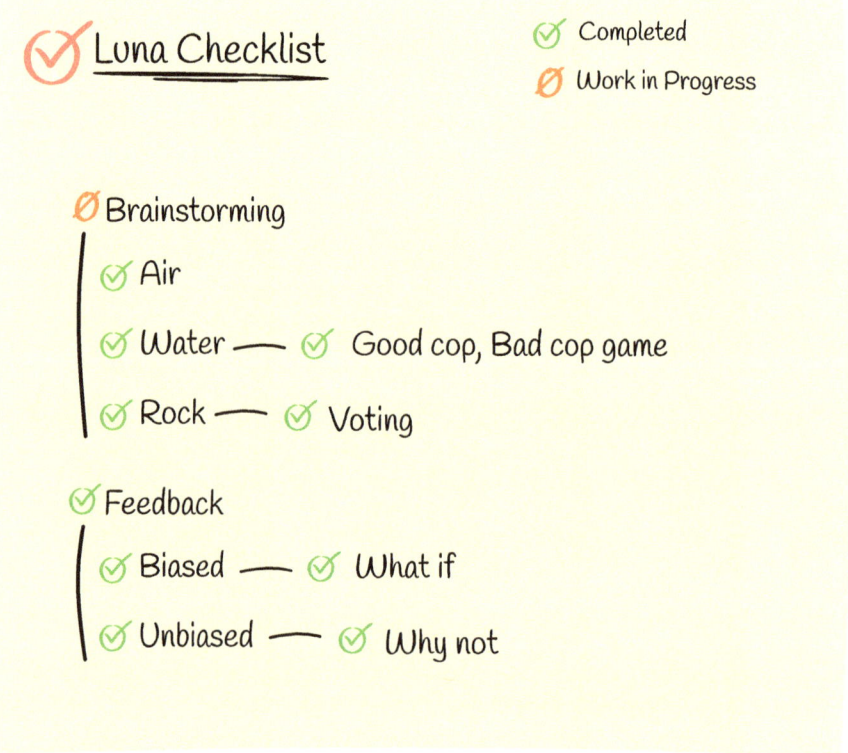

All Gather up!

Expedition #3

Benny Bland

www.bennybland.com

Looks like you really like these case studies!

Let's see how we are doing so far in our checklist!

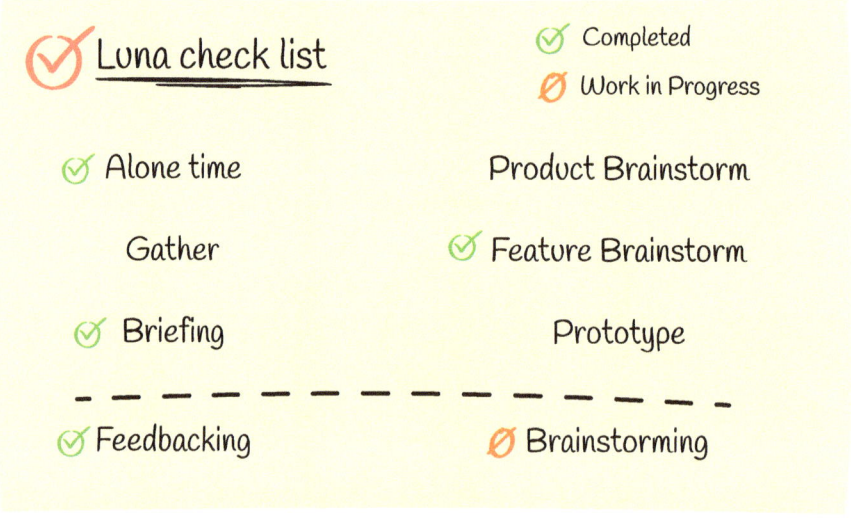

Seems like we did find a couple of points with our first expedition! Now for more!

Too much of information technology going on.
Let's deviate for a bit to avoid overload!

How about something that makes you look fresh...

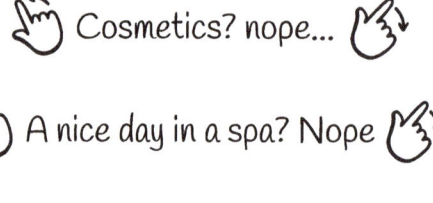

Backdrop

We wanted to treat ourselves and our test users with t-shirts for the amazing work we all doing. you know... something which we could wear with pride!

This was also a passion me and my team shared in common along with stickers!

The "t-shirt" route was accelerated further, as one of my artist was into fashion design before! and frankly sounded a lot more fancy compared to stickers!

 Alright! enough said! Now let's get to work

Hmm... But how?!

We had an idea which was the t-shirt, We also had a few products which we could design the t-shirts for!

So...
- ☑ Idea
- ☑ Design
- ☐ Execution

Something Different

We very enthusiastically placed our product logo over a t-shirt mock up and the product tagline on back of it...

Arranged it a bit... placed a few elements which we thought would go well with the t shirt, like blobs a few wiggly lines and stuff!

Everyone, good job! let's grab something to eat!

After a quick lunch break, we got back to work and we wanted to look at our master piece one more time before we could get to the printing!

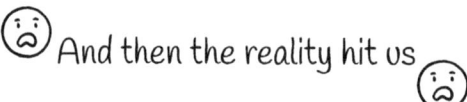 And then the reality hit us

The t-shirt all of a sudden looked so basic and "Bland", we almost ended up in an existential crisis.

So...

- ✓ Idea
- ⦵ Design
- ⊗ Execution

Our faces were filled with confusion and disbelief and we thought to ourselves, how in the world were we so proud of this!

Bland... Oh!

This is where we picked up our name from!
But not yet... this was still the beginning and benny bland was not yet a thing!

Time to shake things up a bit

After we recovered from the shock of the Bland t-shirt.

We grouped up again to decide what we wanted to do with our t-shirt.

The problems at hand:

① We knew it was bland and lacked a sense of personality.

② We did not know how to bring about this personality to it.

Step up

My artist requested a day to think and come up with a design or art which we can use on the t shirt

Tick-tok-tick-tok

After a day of what I assume is them breaking their head to figure out what needs to be done and sketching out tons designs...

 So basically their own "Alone time".

The day after rolled by and they were ready!

We had a look at them, they looked great...
but... still missing something!

They were able to relate to them well because it was their art after all. But, the rest of the team could not really connect!

A gathered Alone time

We decided to all group up and throw in ideas, instead of thinking of it on our own.

We had to add our own flavour to the t-shirt.
So this made a lot of sense to us.

 Everyone gets to contribute something!

A more obvious Approach

☃ The key word for us was Personality

And the most obvious approach was a mascot!

We all pitched in our ideas for greyffiti and feddup on what we think the mascots could be like.

After grilling ourself for a bit, we came up with a mascot for our products.

Off to the drawing board

Once again

☀ This time things were better

The "mascots" looked amazing and when we added them to the t-shirt... they looked great!

Learning from before, we had our lunch and had a look... still great!

♡ So this was final?!

Almost!

Trust the Pessimist

One of the developer told us "this mascot looks too happy."

 Hmm, ok, Please elaborate!

"I was not this happy while fixing all those bugs. I think its great for the product. But, is the happy up beat persona with whom we are planning to go?"

After a quick nervous giggle from the artists and a nervous query whether he was joking...

Which turns out he was not.

After we gave a bit of thought!

We thought it was a fair point

But... But...

Who would really care about a gloomy mascot!

So the Mascots were dropped?

 No absolutely not

They were way too beautiful to let go

We used them for their respective products!

One more version

Before we dispersed to continue with our work, we decided to make a gloomy and a worried version to our otherwise bubbly and happy mascots

 After a couple of hours

We were presented with the gloomy versions of the mascots.

 And...

All of us including the artists hated it.

A Gathering in the clouds

 Time to gather again!

This time... we all wanted to pitch-in and provide the most obvious character trait for our line of work!

✈ Good start...

What now... we were confused...

How do we represent this! we hated the not so bubbly versions! we were stuck!

Ahh..

Nothing striking us.

Foggy minds!

Hmm...

Are you thinking what I was thinking!

Look around and find inspiration!

I was looking around the room... couple of books, files, lots of documents

And...

People... Each with a different emotion, some annoyed, some thinking, some lot in thought!

⚡ This is it! ☀

~~My~~ Our LUNA moment!?

We could make a mascot out of ourselves and make that look gloomy by default! my team loved it!

Now! the points we collected about the character traits would fit perfectly!

And this could be a common mascot for all our products!

When we wanted to represent something which was a little more sarcastic or annoying in nature!

The anxious wait comes to an end

The next day rolled by and my designer unveiled the character

 We were all thrilled

It was perfect!

The right amount of laziness, sarcastic look and an overall annoyed presence!

This was the one, we were going with!

It was almost perfect, we just had to tweak it a bit to make it that much more better!

Say Hello to Benny

We first started of by calling the character "Buddy"...
As he represented a little bit of everyone in the office!

We for some reason, kept calling out to each other with "buddy".

So...

"Buddy, please help me with this"

"Buddy, why is this not working"

And So on...

Now when we were referring to this character "Buddy" repeatedly...

Somewhere along the lines it started to sound more like...

 "Benny"

And we just went with it!

And then... it became his official name!

This was now our:

Core identity   USP

Seems like product brainstorm to Me!

Product Annoy-ification

Now it was time for us to create art with "Benny" in suitable scenarios for our products

What else we got to do?

- We print out the sample benny inspired t shirts for greyffiti and feddup.

- We distribute them:
    - Some for the freelancers
    - Some for the test users
    - Some for ourselves.

An Unexpected twist!

At this point, "benny" was more like a household name in our company.

And I was more or less always wearing my benny inspired t shirt.

So this the twist?

No this is...

One of the day... when I went to meet a person who wanted my team's help with their product.

After our official discussions were done for the day...

😃 Guess what...

One of them asked me about my t shirt!

As they recognised it was my company's product, and wanted to know where we got them designed and printed out...

They wanted to do it for their own product, which was under development!

☺ It was our own design and we printed them near our office! 👋

✉
Now they really wanted one for their product!
♡

Gather with team

When I told this to my designers that this company loved benny and wanted one for them!

We were thrilled.
As this could officially be a thing!

🔑 Remember the keyword is Personality

So me and the designer decided we would spend some time along with them...

...In figuring out how we could represent their product's sarcasm!

Now the Usual...

We designed a couple of samples and a few back and forth... before they could give us the green signal!

A new doubt

The t shirts we did for greyffiti and feddup, were for a closed set of people...

They did not really have any branding beside the product Branding and the main company's branding.

Well...

We can't just add our main companies name to their t shirt!

📣 What now?

Our LUNA moment!
Part 2

We could make our Merchandise line!

And

The name which blured out of us "Benny Bland"

Chef's kiss

This name checked all the boxes!

- ☑ It rhymes
- ☑ It represents what we were thinking
- ☑ It perfectly aligns with the brand identity

This was now our gloomy merchandise's official name!

And "Benny Bland" was born!

All Fired Up!

When we first start with anything, we normally tend to be a lot more enthusiastic and sky is certainly not the limit.

We went wild with the possibilities of Benny Bland

We designed:

- ☀ The logo
- ☀ The theme for the website.
- ☆ Lot more concepts instead of only companies and their product.

What better way to personify anything than comics!

We could make comics on t-shirts!

A new [Starting point] for benny bland.

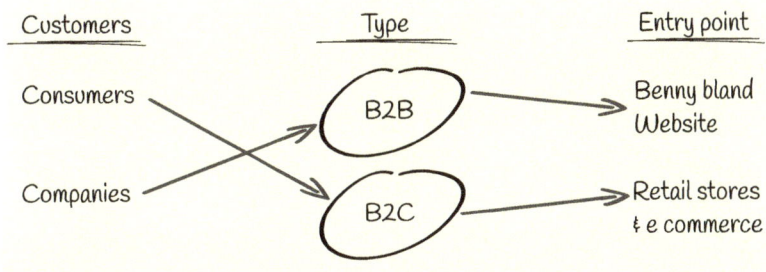

Gather Phase!

Now for getting to work!

But... We did not have a comic artists and my designers were too busy with ample amount of work in hand!

Our Artists introduced us to his friend, who could help create comics for benny bland!

The network is building up! One suggests One more!

We set up a meeting with her and explained the concept and also showed her the previous artworks!

♡ Something new! 👍
She was onboard right from the get go!

Even though a more immediate thing to do we now added "our linking network" step to LUNA.

And thus, this is the tale on how we were able to create our t shirts and utilise our existing Design LUNA processes for non IT related products.

At the same time, add more to the creative cycle of Design LUNA.

It was through the way we used Design LUNA in Benny bland, we were able to:

☼ Engage people in otherwise not so creative departments of my team to provide their inputs.

~AND~

☑ Ideate
☑ Design
☑ Execute

Phew! that was a really really long one!

That only means we get to tick off more from the checklist!

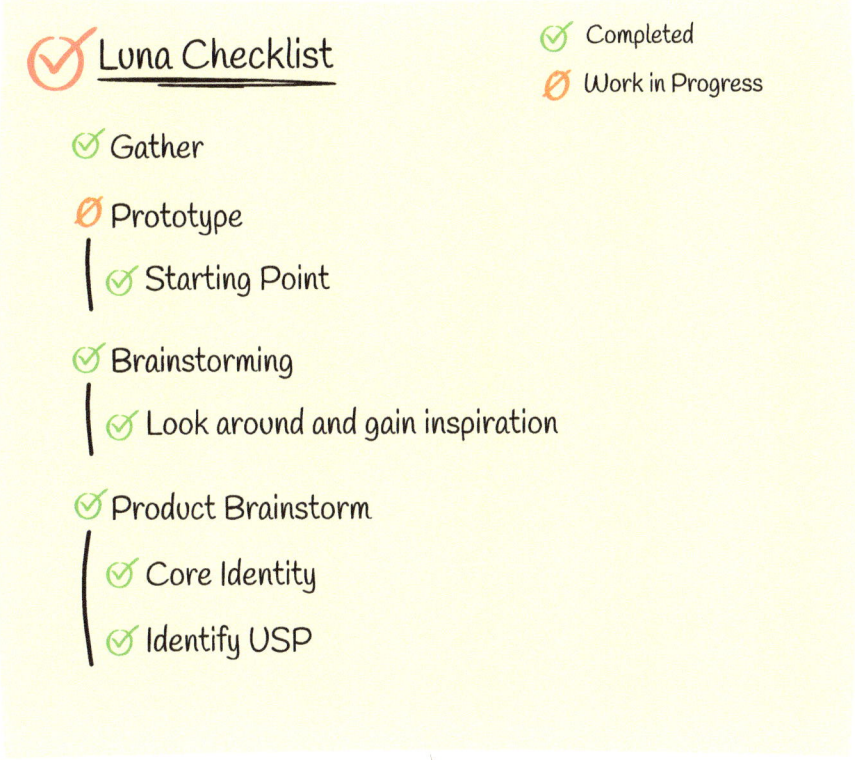

So many waves... Flows!

Expedition #4

Morphline Studio

www.morphline.studio

Ah! our last expedition!

How is our checklist doing so far?

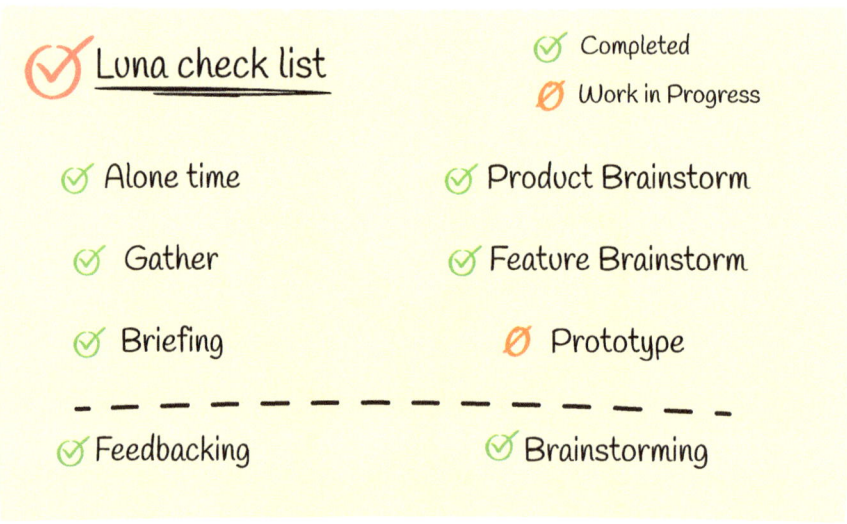

Just a few one more left!

I am pretty sure, this case study will be a great learning experience for you, as much as it was for me!

This is going to be a long one!

Buckle up!

Let's dive right in

 Inception

Wait! don't you mean background? well... this was a start to a new expedition... so.. inception i guess...

Anyways...

During the mid of my startup's journey and product development, I met a lot of people in the due process.

They would ask for assistance in some form or the other, some needed assistance in figuring out a way to do a said thing, some needed potential improvements...

The relation being mutual, I would also ask for some assistance in return. Maybe, a team or an individual that could help me out with a section of my product...

Or

A potential onboarding... if my product seemed to align with their company...

...And...

of course... money if the above were not really materializing

The known Entrepreneur fanatic

We all know of that one friend who REALLY want to be an entrepreneur...

🙌 And wants you in on their billion dollar idea! 💵

For me... this was well not a friend but a father that I met in one of the conferences...

Time to say Hi!

It was a generic business conference along with a couple of speakers and the complimentary dinner so.. yum!

This "father" was speaking with various people and along with this train of speaking with various people, it was my turn...

Here is the gist of it...

We introduced ourselves:

Me:
"Founder and CEO of Threadality technologies, which deals with our own product development as a quick side note Morphline studio"

Morphline studio at the time was primarily focusing on branding, digital art and UI/UX. 🖌

Him:
> "The head of the accounts department in a very well known financial institution and a visiting professor in a reputed institute"

Family Vlogs!

After a few dialogue exchanges on how things are and the normal boring stuff...

⭐ Came the more interesting conversation!

He was there to gain insight on how to formulate and execute an idea his son had!

So where son?

Well... he was in University... couldn't make it to this event. So his father tagged in...

His son had an idea... but, was not really sure how to start it off...

He did a bit of his own intel gathering and remodelling the idea, but something was not really adding up for him.

His father was able to help out with the finances and legalities, but even he hit a road block when it came to execution...

The son's idea

So he was a mechanical engineer and his friends were mostly in that space architects, civil engineers and aeronautical engineers... and of course... mechanical engineers... not a lot of computer science friends...

At that point atleast!

The Idea

The problem that he found was 3 fold:

- ⊗ The equipment that was needed for the course was a bit expensive or not readily available.

- ⊗ The second hand versions were not really maintained that well.

- ⊗ Students were always not sure whether they were buying the right equipment.

☆ I have to add... the university was in the outskirts of the city and e-commerce websites were not really "student friendly" with their delivery rates...

We exchanged our visiting cards and had to decide on a time to meet up and discuss further

Let's dive in

We decided on a time and date to connect with the father – son duo.

This first meeting would be with me.

Once we have the initial discussion and we get on the same boat...

My team would then be looped in.

Story Time

So we started off with understanding the problem statement in greater detail with a story and the problem he faced...

✏️ Stressing on the 3rd point

Not sure wether they were buying the right equipment

 Alright...

- found a problem
- Has a pain point
- Potential solution

🪄 Off to a great start!

I had one question—

There were a lot of shops around the university which sold them for a very low price and the library was pretty good.

So... Equipment it is!

Before we leave

We had a little more discussion about how he would like to move forward with this problem statement and the potential solution...

Which was a Mobile application

where each of the equipment is listed with key information regarding it specifications, image.

Off to my team

My artists were from a really good institute so i thought of speaking with them first to understand how they were able to decide on thier...

As, drawing pads were the only additional "equipment" apart from a laptop which fit this usecase.

 Artist 1:

She just bought an entry level one during start and upgraded alter to a more expensive one after some of her commissioned art pieces made it big...

 Oh! Entrepreneur!

This was great to hear but the key take away was... she bought the device!

 Artist 2:

He leased it from his university until even he bought one for himself...

 Ok this is a useful point...
Let's see what artist 1 has to say!

 Artist 1:

Hello again artist 1

Her university did not offer this facility and everyone had to get their own...

Well... she did say, they some of them just bought iPads as they could it as a laptop and drawing pad

Curiosity Peeked

Now I told them both this was the problem statement along with a paraphrased version of his story and...

The emphasis on the infamous 3rd point

A mobile app was what was needed!

So Tuns out-

It was a problem even they faced when were first starting out...

which was... ▷

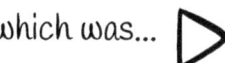 Which drawing pad to buy? ..

Were it's features relevant for the course?

 Was it an over or an underkill? ⚑

✱ A point which I did not think upto this point until my designers raised it...

 They could

Not physically test out or look at this drawing pad

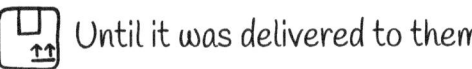 Until it was delivered to them

OK! this is a point which needs to be brought up to him as well

Before we meet

So I asked the "Son" to ask his institute whether they provided the equipment or rented them in anyway...

Meeting 2

It was time to meet with the father and son duo again and this time my artists will be part of the discussion!

It was a problem they had faced first hand so...

Gather phase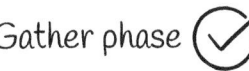

Lot's more value to be added!

So i asked the "Son" to ask his intitue weather they provided the equipment or rented them in anyway

We started off with the problem...

Which my artists faced in finding a drawing pad!

How they had to figure out by themself what works best taking into account-

- ⓘ Cost
- ⓘ Size
- ⓘ Features
- ⓘ Accessibility

etc...

...and the stress on...

NOT being able to physically check the device...

before they bought it!

How to add this to an app now?

this was the question which was raised by him!

We thought, maybe... they could request for a demo and he can give it?

an immediate sarcastic laugh from him followed by

"I have classes to attend as well!"

Let's go step by step

We used "Laptops" as our way to understand the flow...

Now...
I want to buy a laptop so what would I do?

🌐 I could... Check it out on one of the many online stores
✿ Which in our case was NOT really the way to go

~~Or~~

🏪 I could go to a showroom and check out the laptop...

☆

Oh ya! this seemed to be more inline with our "Looking at the equipment before buying" ☆

Hmm... let's expand in this...

Showroom?!

Although a start, we were not really sure where to go with this...

 Place?
- Even if we found it... some one has to be there all day...

- We also need to pay them!

- What if they were on leave, do we close the store or find another?

- Obviously he can't... because... "he had classes to attend!"

Back on the staircase

Well... there are stores where a lot of brands place their stuff... we could do that!

Oh ya! How did we forget this!?!

Where are these showrooms....?

For our usecase.

Many thoughts later...

I looked at the board where we had written our points and realised...

Why not place the equipment there and the book shop guy can take a cut!

Great! so now I put forth this solution...

He was not completely sure whether the book store would allow it...

~~And~~

 A bunch of other problems which we decided to tackle... once we get a green signal from the book stores!

Off he was to speak with them now!

Let's see what materializes!

•
•
•

An anxious couple of days

After about 4 days he got back!

🏪

One of the book store liked the idea and was also ok in storing some ok them equipment as well!

 1...2...3rd party integration

Alright! this seems to be aligning now...

Get it! cause he was a mechanical engineer!

Anyways...

This in hind sight was the easiest thing for us...

Now came the actual problem...

* Who will we get all the equipment?
* How will we keep track of the usage?
* How will we get the word out to the students?

~~AND~~

All the other problems we conveniently kept aside till now...

First issue: Equipment

He prepared a list of the more commonly used ones

↓

We had a look at it

↓

Initial filtering... so, things like scales, compass box and stuff which are not really that difficult to find

↓

Still the list was a little too big!

↙

Time to ask the experts

We thought, he could ask his professor about what equipments are really needed from this updated list

And also

○

...Even though we were really worried about the number we would hear...

 We wanted to know about the number of students in each year who were enrolled in mechanical, civil and architecture.

If the professor does not know

 Ask someone who could give us a ballpark number atleast!

A few more anxious couple of days

Now it was time to review all the information we collected

The equipment list was much smaller

That is Great!

As expected... the students were too many!

We decided that we would not really count in the students who were in their penultimate or final year.

And

We would focus mostly on freshers

But...

The number was still pretty big! buying or even leasing all this equipment would be very expensive!

How about take some money from students to buy equipment?

Not sure... Why would they trust us yet!

So after a little bit of the father - son duo working on the math

The father was willing to buy about 30 equipment max to kick start this...

Wow ok! a much better number than we expected!

But we will be needing more...

So we thought "Son" could get some of his friends or maybe even the professor on board to be part of their venture...

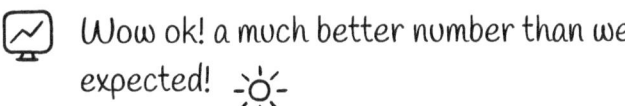

This was our version of Talent Acquisition

Smooth sailing upto this point...

Now it's time to figure out the main problem

Equipment? = channel strategy

Although we were a little hesitant... Buying the equipment in MRP was the priority :|

What about buying them from seniors?

- ↻ Wasn't that the first problem... that they might not be maintained that well...
- ↻ Won't the equipment be old as well...

But the MRP could not be our only avenue...

💎 This was an interesting development... One which they had to gather more intel on after the meeting

Now with-
- 🎯 One avenue set
- 🎯 The other one in a maybe state

Now it was time to

Cue the book store

We were in the intel gather part of the discussion... so, we thought of figuring out what more intel had to be gathered

And

 Book Store it is!

First off...
We had to collect info on

- When he and his peers visited the book store
- When they visited the library

Once this was out of the way...

The "Son" along with the "Friends onboarded"

Could stand near these location and get the people around preferably seniors to

Sell their equipment to them at a fair rate

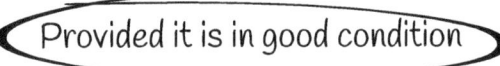

And... Of course..

 These channels underway to begin with

More once we establish!

Now show time

Alright! now it was time for them to get to work...

Off... me and my team were in doing our work as usual.

Now, it was time for "The son" to get back after he felt things shaped up to a certain extent...

After about a month or 2

- ⚙ He got 4 friends onboard

- ⚙ The professor could not because of conflict of interest by the way!   *He was ready to help if required*

- ⚙ They were able to get around 70 of various equipments from channels we had decided.

🖅 Now its time to tackle the next issues

We first set our sight on

Operational flow

We had to figure out the answers to these questions...

- ⏏ How are we going to collect money?

- ⏏ How do we split the money with the book store?

- ⏏ How are we going to make sure the equipment is returned?

- ⏏ What are we planning to do – if they misplace or brake the equipment in anyway?

Alright... let's go one after the other...

How are we going to collect money?

Also

How do we split the money with the book store?

Well they are similar...

So the Idea was...

A QR code which could be scanned with an application like Google pay or Samsung pay

After that... every month end all the bills and the usage from the admin portal will be

Collected
↓
Tallied
↓
Settled

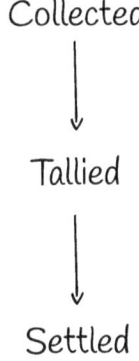 It is important to note that:

This was NOT a registered firm...

So... Going completely automated would not really be feasible!

Ok Next stop...

How do we make sure equipment is returned?

 The institute's library had one way of doing it, where if any book is not returned its just added to your fees before you leave.

 Now these guys can't really do that

How do the book stores do it?

 Just give them a call or message them that the book is due today or the due has passed...

and with every passing day a late fee is added...

This seemed like the way to go ∿

But the main problem still remained...

What if they just don't return the equipment?

Going with trust would really work out!

3rd Party ~~Integration~~ Improvisation

The "Son" told why not ask the head security guard if they could help...

📅 Once the due date has passed 📄

The details of the student like their:

1. Name

2. ID number

Would be shared with guards and when the said student scans the ID card at the exit gate...

A security guard could stop the student and make sure the property is retuned...

👍 Brilliant! This would do! 🙌

Broken or misplaced

Now the last one...

What if the equipment is misplaced or broken?

It was decided the student needs to pay full price for the new equipment and that's pretty much it!

So if they can buy a new equipment as a replacement!

Also...

To ensure no miscommunication...

An image of the equipment would be taken by both the store and the person renting it.

On return, they would be compared to see if a fine is required

Operation flow ✓

Analyse the store

Now it was time for market analysis...

Here's what we had to figure out...

- 💲 How much we had to ask from the students?

- 💲 How much we had to give the book store?

- 💲 If the security would take a portion in this as well?

And...

Renting strategy

It was now time for the group of friends to ask around and collect all the data using which we could create a plan...

Filled with data

Once they finished asking around and done with their exams and all things in between...

We connected again after a month

Here were their findings:

- Most of the students received a pocket money of some sort from their parents for their expenses

- No one really had a financial split, but they did keep this book renting in mind

- Quite a few of them were really interested in renting out the equipment instead of buying it at least in the first few semesters

Coming to the renting...

After asking a lot of students the average they found was "3 weeks".

So an average of around 3 week an equipment would be rented...

Daily seemed scary to most and monthly would not work...

Weekly

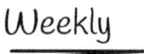

Seems to be the most optimal

Ok Now...

How much we had to give the book store?

The book store was expecting around 35% of the monthly revenue

What about the security guard?

The security guard was expecting a small sum of money

So...

If a student was identified they would go out of their way by making sure...

Equipment was retuned to the store

Or

Given to a security guard

On the same day

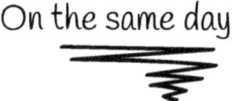

An Important blank

This information was great but still did not answer one crucial question...

How much we had to change the student per week?

Looking into how the book store operated, we decided on...

On charging 15% of the MRP of the equipment...

This would make sure the price is less... at the same time would allow them to buy more equipment as well down the line!

⚡ Alright now... ☁️

2 more to go:

- Development strategy
- Customer acquisition

We decided to go parallel with these ↗↗

Customer Acquisition

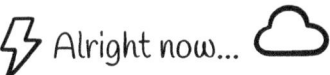 My artists made a fancy logo and some designs for standees

Which they can print and place in the book store and few pamphlets which could be handed out

As a little bit of a gimmick

 ~And~

Also to prove some more information

The number of equipments currently available would be written on one of the standees...

Development strategy

As we were designing logo and pamphlets

The group of friends were figuring out where to print the pamphlets and get a standee...

In the mean time, we decided...

The book store could use a register to note down all the information manually... Until...

They go all electric with...

The admin portal!

New found motivation

 With a new found motivation and inspiration...

By the way we were progressing with this idea!

 One of the "Onboarded friend" who was studying computer science wanted to build this application.

 Morphline studio can help him out with any queries or assist him in testing out the application!

 Seems fair!

Why not go for it!

 This could also be added to his resume later on...

So win-win!

What needs to be developed

 Admin Portal which shows:

- Equipment name
- Weekly rental price
- Specifications

Once a student rents a device

- Student's name
- Student's ID number
- Student's Phone number
- Date taken
- Return date

For student...

A web application which is mobile friendly...

Where they can scan a unique QR code pasted on the equipment case to check information like-

- Equipment Specifications
- Date rented
- Date to return
- Weekly rental rate

A similar melody

 It was now their time to get all of this ready and up and running

Now for me and my team, it was time to unearth the gold mine we discovered in the due course of this engagement with them...

An amazing tale on how they were able to go from...

From
LOST

to

design LUNA

this is the really really long tale on how we were able to quite literally build the other half of LUNA

Well looks like we have checked off all the boxes!

Ok! that was lot of reading!

I am pretty sure you had a

Enough of my company using Design LUNA

Let's look at others Journeys as well

Destiny:

Design LUNA

Journey #1

Glitters on the mirror

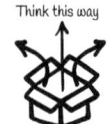 Yay! LUNA makes more friends!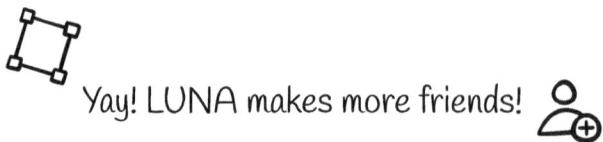

Let's see how they were able to use Design LUNA and

 Think outside the box

Before we start

⚠️ Spoiler Alert ⚠️

An App is not always the solution!

~~Background~~ Context

As part of Threadality, we help businesses in coming up with solutions to a problem statement, or if they have a solution, we help streamline it or enhance it further!

And Guess what we use

Ofcourse you guessed it!

So, what about this Now?

One of our clients of Morphline studios, was facing a challenge of some sort.

During one of my visit... he told me about this particular problem they were facing.

OK! What was this problem

Before I tell you about the problem, you need to know what is that they do...

This is a jewellery boutique, which specialises in making beautiful ornaments with various precious stones.

They follow a very interesting and intricate process

Where they set up a meeting with the client and understand 2 important things, which help in designing the ornament:

- The occasion

- The client's emotional connect with the occasion

With these two points, they along with the client identify key factors to create a story on...

Once they have a good idea, the team set out to create a one off ornament set which tells the tale of this client and brings about a journey on its own...

So each set is:

 Unique and is not replicated

 Really Really expensive

Now for the problem

At last...

The clients need to see this piece in a way which is better than a sketch or a blueprint!

and it should be clear enough to be able to suggest changes if any...

And most importantly

Get a feel for the ornament

A little sneaky but worth it

I had visited the boutique a couple of times...

In these visits, I had the opportunity to interact with various members of the team.

I was always fascinated and wanted to bring about the below observations to my firm as well-

- 📌 Their ability to identify key elements in narrating the clients story.
- 📌 Team of people who are really motivated and passionate about the work they do.
- 📌 Also, the story telling capabilities of the sales executives.

which is often looked over...

↑↑↑↑ So many parallels with

Design LUNA

Here's why:

- They were really good at "feature brainstorming", as they hit a home run every time in identifying key narration points.

- They were actively seeking feedback before they get to the actual work.

- A close knit team, so... gather phase was already well in its work.

Let's do things a little different

 I suggested... "Why not try out design LUNA..."

And stated the plethora of things which were already in play...

 Why not engage the rest...

Gather up

 After a little bit of discussion... I received the green signal!

 Now its time to Design LUNA!

No... it was time to:

Set up meeting date   Meeting place

As, our emphasis was on the gather phase...

We decided on one of the meeting rooms in the workshop, where we had sufficient place for the key team members.

We then set out to "Gather" people within the company with varied backgrounds and experience.

Some new to the game and some veterans in this field!

The LUNA bootcamp

We decided on a 3 day training period before they could go ahead and figure out the solution to their actual problem!

Now... Now... its time to Design LUNA!

The best way to learn is by doing...

So we brought out all the required accessories which Design LUNA demands:

- Board
- Pens paper
- Clock
- Necklace mannequin — *This acted as the talking stick!*

And all the other stuff to simulate the real thing as much as we possibly could.

Now that we are all set up...

We started off by making a list of sample problem statements.

We made sure these were in no way related to the actual problem they were trying to solve..

Something similar to the delivery app which is in this book.

In all honesty, this was the most difficult step for all of us

Once we were able to jump over this...it was a breeze...

We then decided that each would be the facilitator for their topic...

This would allow everyone to exchange roles and be more proactive in other's ideas as well!

Bootcamping with LUNA

First, me explaining a topic in LUNA

followed by a quick Q and A.

Figuring out how it applies to their own sample problem

Now the best part

A deeper dive, where they actually get to experience the LUNA phases...

In the due process, any queries can be clarified right away!

Another upside 📈

Each of these sample problem statements brought up were quite different from each other

so the quires and confusions were quite different and they were able to get a wholistic picture!

 Showtime!

🚀 Now the bootcamp is done!

The sample problem statements tackled with!

Cheers everywhere for the amazing job!

📈 Tomorrow onwards it is the real deal!

As they need to figure out a solution for their actual problem! 💡

The next day rolls by and everyone assembles..

First off, who will be the facilitator?
Well... that would be the owner of the Boutique
Alright so... facilitator ✓

Next stop:

Each of the participants suggest 1 or 2 more people

The bootcamp was predominantly done with:
- Head of staff
- Head of Sales
- Lead designer... jewellery designer
- Boutique Managers
- Of course... the owner

Hmmm... Lot's of bosses... they may or may not have too much interactions with the clients...

So now it was time for them to gather the members who work more closely with the customers.

Alright so... Gather few more people ✓

Ok! looks like they were all set!

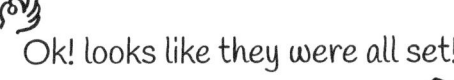

My job was to only observe

And

If things got a bit interesting... add some more points or improvements to LUNA

Now the real show begins

The problem statement which was the one, that had to be actually discussed, was written on their glass board...

♡ I really liked that glass board

Back to the topic...

After the briefing phase was done!

Now off they went about throwing all possible ideas, some from the boutique manager, some from the designer, and some from the owner himself...

👍

It was fun seeing them occasionally look back at their notes to check whether they were on the right track

As the session progressed, they got increasingly more critical in their thinking and identifying aspects of problems. These would otherwise not be brought up if it was not for the diverse group of participants.

Hey! Nice statement man

Ok... Let me elaborate...

At the very beginning of the case study I alerted you of a spoiler which was...

App is always not the answer 📱

let's see why...

One of the participants' who was a junior designer... so a lot more in tune with today's technology trends, suggested that an Augmented Reality (AR) application would be a good way to showcase designs.

⌜I am⌟ pretty sure while you read through the problem statement in the beginning, this might have struck you as well! 🎤

 So moving on...

The designer took out his phone and showed a couple of videos on some AR apps and also downloaded an AR game...

This further hyped up the crowd and they really wanted this to be the way to go...

So why was this not the one which was green lit?

Hmm... let's see...

Remember Good cop - Bad cop

Although not a setup for good cop bad cop...

This discussion took a turn due to the earlier training alignment!

Where the participants were trying to better understand the way it works... slowly turned into the good cop bad cop...

So at this point the group was divided into 2 sets:

Yes AR app   No AR app

It was in the due process of disagreements and bringing up possible limitations within the technology...

Amidst all of this excitement, they realized...

3D art was not even part of their work flow!

Which was the foundation of Augmented Reality!

At present, the ornaments were drawn by hand

For each of the stones, a marking was made and each section was drawn separately.

The client was shared a detailed version of the same and their feedback was recorded!

Good cop Bad cop doing good things

The 3D models for the jewels came as a bit of a blow

But nothing to panic... this was just a minor inconvenience along the way...

Now it was time for the good cop to step up ↑

One of them suggested recruiting a 3d artist

V̊ A tackle from the bad cop

"Not very easily available"...

A more favourable path

"How about freelancers?"

Great! Now, the Head of Staff was off to find 3D artists on various freelancing portals and speak with few known connects.

🎉 After a bit... he found a few 3D artists!

Yay! They were all back to cheers! 😃

📱 Yay! AR application!

Well not quite :(

Looming problems

Everyone has that one person in their team who is a bit of a pessimist...

In this scenario, it was the owner who amidst all this discussion got a very valid question which steered the conversation again...

After checking for answers online and downloading a few apps and playing around with them

 Anti Eureka Moment!

He noticed, NONE of the AR apps and games worked, if they were projected on any surface other than a flat one!

Up to this point, all of them were fascinated by the cool games and application...

And everyone skipped over this point when they were first trying out the apps...

They would work only when projected on the table or the office floor!

AR not augmenting

As the amount of time spent to find a 3D artist was quite a lot. An idea around 3D was still on the cards.

Now it was time for another buzzing technology trend

 3D printing!

This was now seeming lot more hopefull

Printing Dreams!

So now a new groups were formed:

Yes 3D printing

No 3D Printing

Some of them infact had done some 3D printing before and were very quick to not really be all-in on this idea!

Once each of them did their research, questions like:

> ? Where will we be getting them printed from?

> ? Our ornaments are detailed pieces... so will a generic printer be able to print it?

> ? Where will we get a 3D printer from?

> ? Will revisions on 3D models and printing be cost effective?

 And most importantly

Many of them were not really convinced with the quality of the final product and the amount of work needed to make it look good!

Ah well! seems like this dream was a little short lived

○ ○ ○ Seems like they hit a road block ○ ○ ○

Look around...

Just like almost all of the greatest inventions ever...

Their potential solution was also discovered as an

 Accident!

In one of the corners of the room was a storage cabinet...

That had glass doors ⟶ and on those doors were

Fancy Etchings

Oh! looks like they found it!

Although, the idea seemed very simple and silly!

Also, they were...

 literally writing on a glass board!

But the sales executive who suggested this idea, was adamant for them to give it a try!

She ran to the store and got a mirror which they used
for clients to look at the finished product

↓

Requested the lead designer to sketch something out!

↓

Designer grabbed a few markers on the table

↓

Started to sketch out a necklace

↓

Sketch completed... now it was...

🎁 **Time to unveil this masterpiece**

It was made with white board markers so, kind of... off...

But every one were able to see the potential in this.

How about... print the necklace in a transparent sheet and stick it on the mirror.

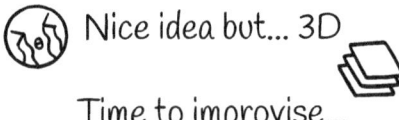 Nice idea but... 3D

Time to improvise...

Now it was time to try it with pencils that were made specifically to write on glass, and to draw the ornament instead...

 Hmm... interesting!

I am pretty sure you must have seen these pencils being used by a carpenter!

As an added bonus for this team...

These pencils came in some different colors as well

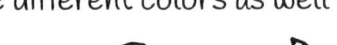

Next big day

Next day, the designer bought a few pencils of different colors to match a couple of the precious stones...

The necklace was drawn again...

It looked a lot more believable but still looked... off.

After everyone had a staring contest with the sketched out necklace...

The Head of Marketing told the designer to draw this on one of the bigger mirrors...

The idea being, maybe if they were viewing it from a little far it would be a lot more convincing...

Third time is the charm

Now for the 3rd time... designer drew the necklace!

This time along with a staring contest they started to figure out the perfect position to align themselves with the necklace...

 They all lit up!

They found the way to do it! :)

It was detailed enough for the client to get an idea and also for them to suggest changes, if they needed any!

 Jackpot!

Where was I in all of this

 Like a bird watcher just looking around and noting things down..

Not interfering in their discussion!

 But...

One thing I must confess...

I was really happy when they did not go with the app idea... It makes things a little less fun!

○
○
○

So well, this was a tale on how a company started with an obvious solution and ended up with something that was achievable in a short period of time!

Wait, So what about the 3D models

OK, they were going with it but a little later...

They wanted to showcase the ornaments as 3D renders instead of 3D print and AR applications.

Atleast to start off with...

That was a lot to read!

No!!

 Alright! 👍 ✈

Let's embark on an other journey!

🚢

Journey #2

Back to school!

 Time for LUNA to learn a thing or two!

This was a real fun for me especially, as it was a new experience...

Something different from the usual work...

Let's get started!

Chapter 0

So, my father's ex-colleagues sometimes organize family get-togethers when everyone is free or in the same country...

Nothing too fancy, most of the times its just meeting in a restaurant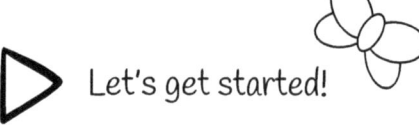

The adults get to catch up on life and work

The kids get to play around...

I guess...

I normally won't really bother to go to these "get togethers"

⭐ BUT this year it was a little special! 😁

A very close friend of my father whom I have known since my childhood and who has also helped me a lot during my initial days of my startup journey was joining in..

🚗 So... I had to tag along this time

The big day!

We were all ready to meet him...

We had a lot of catching up to do!

⏱️ And more so

I had to tell him about all the amazing stuff we were up to...

The products we were building, the fun new tool we had developed, the procedures we follow...

and of course...

Design LUNA!

Hi's & Hello's

We meet at last...

⏱ We spoke for hours about all the amazing stuff my startup was up to and all the previously mentioned talking points!

And then... ✈

We naturally had to speak with others as well 👶 which is fine I guess, nothing really out of the ordinary...

Tummies grumbling

Me, my father sat along with him to grab something to eat... 🍽

 Well... there was a lot more to talk after all...

All that was not possible during the first wave of our discussion.

This time we dwell a lot more deeper with our discussion...

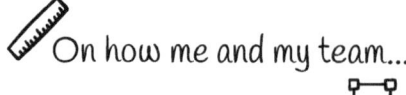

Formulate our products

 Design solutions for our clients

 Fun ways we get our team members engaged

 As part of the dialogue, some of the elaborate art pieces my artists have done for our products and also for our clients

Not so top secret mission

 Listening to all of my ramble...

The occasional pitching in from my father to tell him about his contributions and viewpoints on some of the decisions made and course of actions...

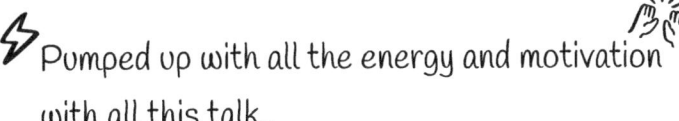 Pumped up with all the energy and motivation with all this talk..

 Now came the time where we get to brainstorm something together!

Idea from inconvenience

So...

He recently attended a workshop/ seminar conducted by his office to ensure the staff is up to date with

- The latest technology trends
- To figure out ways in which they will be able to incorporate their new learnings into the company's existing flows

Well...

 He was not really a fan of how the sessions were laid out

Why you ask?

Because of

Time constraints   Flow of modules

Main issue

Some of the core topics were just brushed over...

 As they believed, the people taking part in this training would be well versed in said topics

 So... in the end everyone came out with lot more questions than answers.

Now it's time to...

Start his own training institute!

No! seriously this was the IDEA...

Now that our story time is done...

So do we get to work?

Well yes!

First off... our initial gather phase was done!
$\qquad$ To a certain extent

 The friend: He was part of the training faculty for many corporate training programs and was also a trainer in couple of training institutes.

 My father: Not in the training side of things... but he had helped design courses and their material for many companies, universities and training institutes!

Hmm... ok... and... You?

Glad you asked...

 Obviously, I don't have the level of experience these guys had...

BUT...

I certainly had was the new age understanding on how these things worked...

I had attended so many seminars, conferences, training programs and events which made my view points a lot more broader than being stuck with the corporate way of looking at things

Also...

Me and my team had started a program called "En4ce"

Where we taught underprivileged students of varying ages; computers sciences and stuff!

This allowed me to add a different perspective and that personal touch as well! ♡

How do we get started?

First, I had to get one question out of the way...

Why not just continue with the training institutes you were already a part of?

No flexibility and opportunity to shake up the syllabus while teaching the format is too rigid and too strict with timelines!

 A Natural second question...

Who are you planning to train?

○
○
○

Students who are new to the job market, people trying to change career path and working professionals who are trying to take their knowledge to the next level!

 OK!

A very Bold and Encouraging statement

 Follow up question...

What exactly are you going to train them in?

Predominantly IT related courses but with a focus on financial tools and services!

 Made sense... He was in the banking and finance industry from the longest of time

Now the main question...

This was more of a self motivated one...

I will let you know 'why' in a bit...

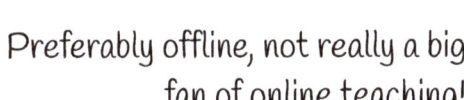

 I was noticeably happy after this answer!

I was not really a big fan of online learning myself!

 Same book for sure...

But are we on the same page?

 Time to counter argue!

Well online is easier to start off with not a lot of set up involved, no need to rent out a place, desks, chairs, network and others...

Please don't change your stance...

○
○
○

Ya but... I think it's a lot more engaging if it is physical and I could be able to understand the room better, rather than just assuming everything is alright when in an online setting

Yay! thank god he did not make the switch!

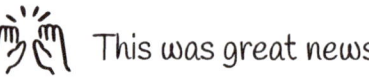 This was great news!

We certainly were on the same page may be even alphabet!

But now...

○
○
○

How do we rent out these places to conduct the training sessions

○
○
○

Ahh! well... it's a problem for later...
Let's tackle something else for now!

1.0.1 or 2.3.9?

Now time to tackle

Now.... off my father and the friend were to...

Decide on a bunch of open source tools, programming languages, software which needed to be included and taught in the courses

In the due course of the unfolding discussion

Came a tool which my father had not heard of before and it was free... so why not download it!

That task was given to me...

I did have my laptop... well, I had to show the amazing stuff we were working on afterall...

1) Laptop ✓

2) Website where I can download this software from ✓

3) This is where the problem arises...

There were too many versions and releases...

I could figure out the version but was really confused with the release part...

Some had new features, some had features which were part of the older ones but not really working as intended and...

OK wait! time to get back and just ask them...

Well! what do you know...

He told me in an instant;
Pointing at the screen that this is the version and release I need to install!

 OK! that was faster than I expected!

A slight change in course

I was a little confused...

? Was this something the students were supposed to know?

? Was this something they have to figure out for themselves?

And... I did ask them about the same

No, we will be teaching them this part as well...

Ok but...

How is this something they are going to know before hand...

How are they going to understand that this is something which is needed for the job that they are working towards...

Hmm...
An unexpected turn of events as...

This basically tickled down to a basic question

Where are we going to get the students from?

A new trip to start with

We halted the course content side of stuff for a bit and set out to figure out...

Who   How

We are trying to train!

Lot's of...

 "Corporate"

Being thrown around!

So taking my changes...

Why not start with companies, you guys worked in! maybe, that could be a good starting point!

I could not have been more wrong

 I was immediately bombarded with...

No! Too many processes involved to get through

Too many approvals

We are just starting off...
so... No balance sheet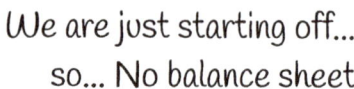

 And they just kept going...

Reading the room

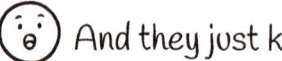 Guess I got to take the hint...

Corporate was off...

...For now at least!

Anyways this time... Well more like observing the room...

The people who attended this get-together...

- Some, who were working in pretty big companies!

- Few, who had their own firms!

- A couple of them, who were freelancers or consultants!

- A good number of them came with their children, who were studying computer science in university!

Well this seems convenient...

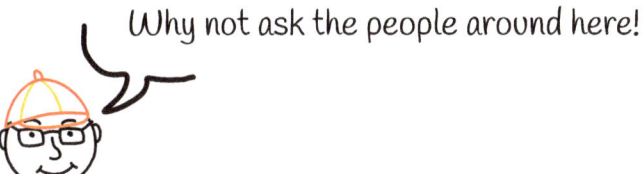

Now...

The three of us created a list of questions...

That I could go around and ask each of the individual about... things like...

- What you would like to learn?

- If you were in a position to tell your team members to learn how would that go.

- What do you think is causing a disconnect between new recruits and people already working in the firm.. skill or knowledge wise...

And a few more...

Seems familiar right...

This was our journalist feedback-ing phase!

 Wait...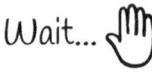

What did you guys brainstorm to get to this phase?

Well our initial product brainstorm was on in deciding the course content

Until

I got confused installing the software!

Now that the questionnaire was completed!

 Off I went to ask people around

 ...And...

They chit-chat... I guess!

I enter the scene again

After a good amount of time...

Asking the known people around these questions

Noting their responses

Now... I was back to share my finding with them...

I did not ask everyone, of course!

?

Remember, the "Negotiator phase" is left!

Now we storm again this time it was my father and his friend...

They were discussing on the points which I collected

I was observing what the counter arguments were... if it was up my ally, I would give my 2 cents as well!

After a lot of discussions
...And...
A lot of Back and forth

☆ The updated set of questions with counter arguments were ready!

Now I have a handbook of counter arguments as well

 This would help me to strike a more compelling dialogue with the people I am talking with!

The same tango... Again

First...
I have to speak with the people I did NOT
During the first wave of interaction....

Also update and add some more points to my counter argument bank and of course note down the findings

This was my Unbiased crowd

Once speaking with this group is done

 "Hello again" to the previous group!

Now this time they were my

 Who turned into a

Unbiased crowd   Biased crowd

This is a fun little observation when I had interacted with them (the previous group) the second time around!

Back to it again!

Now...

The new set of points were studied and discussed!

→ This time I was a lot more engaged...

↳ As I had gained a good amount of insight and I could draw parallel with my experience!

👉 While we were debating amongst ourselves and figuring out what points need to be given more importance...

When we looked at it in a wider perspective we noticed the patterns which hid in plain sight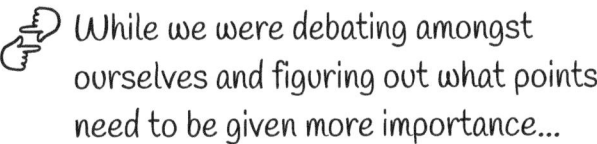

Here is what we noticed:

 Corporates:

- They wanted to ensure the candidate's basics are really strong.
- Understand more about the testing side of stuff

Consulting firms:

✓ They were a different ball game altogether

- They wanted to conduct workshops and seminars instead
- The people who newly joined their team will be part of this "teaching" program

 This is an interesting development...

We thought this could be added in right away to

 The courses brochures and marketing materials!

 Students:

- They wanted to be trained the application side of the programming language rather than the theoretical side as this was already being covered by their university!
- Find avenues to apply their theoretical knowledge

 I saved the best best for last!

Under startups we were able to categorize them into two section

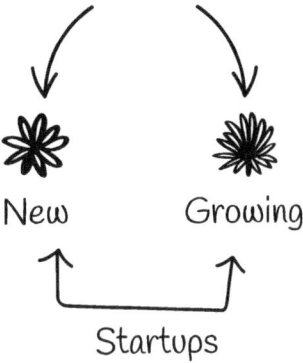

 Were the ones most interested in this...

it could give them...

→ The initial boost they require...

→ Could help with their startup's branding

→ The seasoned professionals who are associated with this new startup can focus on products features and stuff.

 They were leaning towards what the consultants had stated where the startup members could conduct seminars and stuff to boost their firms popularity!

So...

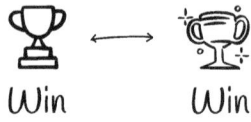
Win   Win

 Growing startups...

Close second place in the...

 "Interested in the idea" leaderboard

→ They were not really interested in getting people trained in the stacks they knew little about... mostly because they would not be recruited in the first place

Hey! This is a good proposal for the students...

                                   Let's note it down real quick

→ they wanted their candidate to enhance their current skill, which would boost the firm's productivity.

So the topics which they were looking at were more in the lines of optimization, collaboration and pipelining...

 With a dash of trending technologies that were not tried and tested yet... but gaining traction

Guess Who?

From the above description it should certainly not come as a surprise that...

...where who we wanted to target first!

OK! our customer acquisition for the first phase was set!

Now a quick "closer" phase

Before we get to

Development strategy

So we knew the entry point

People who are working in startups who are planning to up their skills

We have our customer acquisition which is from the new startups and growing startups!

 Why should they choose us?

How to make the people involved happy?

What makes us happy?

When we get what we want... I guess!

In this context...

What's better than being part of designing a curated course, which aligns with your firms requirements!

 And that is what we went with...

 We create a basic skeletal structure for the course...

 Sit along with the startups we are onboarding, to put forth their requirement.

⚓ Decide the level importance on the modules and topics

↓

☃ Come up with a skeletal timeline

↓

✈ Verify timelines with startups

↓

👍 Green signal from Startups!

🏭 Well great! 🎯
Let's get to the training!

Are you sure? Something's missing right?

🏪
Ah! Yes of course how do we rent a place...

😜 Let's postpone this again... 🕒

It's already too late, we got to go back home from this get-together! 🚌

 After a couple of days...

 A fresh mind and clear of mental blocks

Here were each of our problems:

> Startups are too spread apart and finding a common location for all would not really be possible...

> Even if we find place, the set up cost for things like desks, internet connection, projectors and other equipment would be too high

> Well I had a different problem all together... I had just completed my university course and was back... so I had no interest in a classroom style setup!

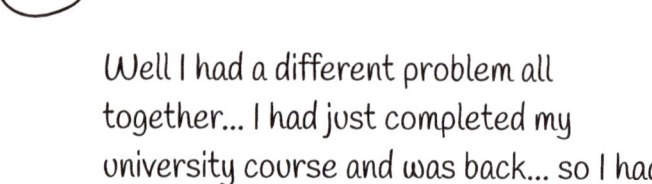

ⓘ So each of us had our own problem...

So let's figure out what can be done... 🔗

Connecting the dots

Third ∞ Party ∞ Integration!

the problem still remains... integrate What? ~~~~

Desk and stuff would still be "high initial cost"

...and...

My "classroom" setup problem is not solved

Look around the room again... 📺

 Well more like looking into...

The conferences, events and meetups I was part of...

Where did I attend events in the past:

 University campuses...
Their amphitheater

✗ This seems unlikely ✗

 Company's
- Meeting rooms
- Common areas

These meetups had table chairs, projectors and stuff...

Ahh! no they look like classrooms...

✗ This seems unlikely ✗

I also attended some in...

Wait 🖐

Before I revel this, a quick word association

We were looking at ↙
⋮
↓
Startups
⋮
↓
Startups are known for collaboration...
⋮
↓
What better place to collaborate than
⋮
↓
Co-working spaces

The events which were conducted here were...

-  Lot more easy flowing
-  Had an open atmosphere
- 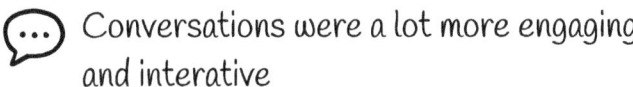 Conversations were a lot more engaging and interative

And...No classroom Feel!

Oh! ya, the best part...

 Beanbags!

A more fun way to get your work done!

Or in this case...

Get trained!

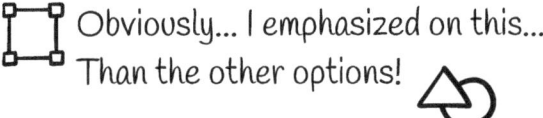 Obviously... I emphasized on this... Than the other options!

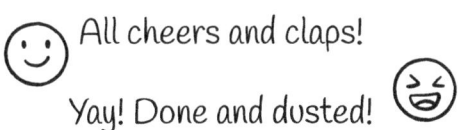 All cheers and claps! Yay! Done and dusted!

After the initial eureka phase...
Phased out...

? The question was...

Meetups that you attended were for a day or 2 at max would this be useful if it would go for weeks on end?

Hmm... ya... Point!

The obvious solution mix of both!
Add in a bunch of desks... sit on what ever you please!

Considering you were a student when you attended these meetups... beanbags for experienced professionals!? seems kiddish... right?

Well not a problem... They could pull in more desks from the co-working space. Problem solved!

Wait, what about location?

Co-working spaces are everywhere these days.. especially in and around universities and offices!

Great! Each of our problems were solved!

Location ✓

Reduced setup cost ✓

A little bit of a fun environment! ✓

Now what?

Now it was time for the friend to run around!

Collect the data which is required
↓
Speak with a couple of startups
↓
Get them on board

Later on...

He and my father would decide on:

- The course content
- The important modules which have to be included
- Duration of the course
- Dash of up and coming technologies!

---Once this is done---

Speak with the onboarded startup!

Now... 😢

Our journey has truly come to an end :(

So many

Expeditions   Journeys

We have embarked on!

I am sure you have learned a lot from them!

New IDEA? Think the LUNA way!

About me

www.threadality.com

Hi! I am Mukundh Bhushan. I am the founder and CEO of Threadality Technologies!

Tagging along with the stories of many... I started my first IT business out of my college dorm room, at the age of 19.

As expected, I had to do everything on my own!

Not the most optimal way... but a great way to start! for me at least :)

I had to teach and train myself in navigating the space that is "entrepreneurship"...

 I am really excited to pen this book down and take you along with me on this amazing and ongoing journey... which is my startup!

 From learning how to get out there and showcase my work, recruiting the right set of people for the job, manage and motivate my team... most importantly... and relevant to this book... how to think... think efficiently!

www.ingramcontent.com/pod-product-compliance
Ingram Content Group UK Ltd.
Pitfield, Milton Keynes, MK11 3LW, UK
UKHW060213240426
12048UKWH00031BB/1711